"So...

what I

REALLY meant..."

"So...
what I
REALLY meant..."

Better Communication

Better Relationships

Alison Poulsen, PhD

No book, including this one, can replace the services of a qualified health professional.

ISBN 978-1500592493

Published by RLM Publishing
Alameda, CA 94501

Printed in the United States of America
Published in 2014.

sowhatireallymeant.com

CONTENTS

ACKNOWLEDGMENT

I wish to thank the readers of my blog who have opened their hearts and shared their personal challenges. I am grateful to each individual who has come to me for counseling to improve their relationships and their wellbeing.

I would like to thank my exceptional friend Heather King for her innovative thinking and coming up with the title and concept of my blog and this book.

I would like to thank my immensely talented sister Mimi Stuart for allowing me to use her art to enrich my blog and for designing the book cover. She has also provided many helpful edits and witty ideas that are biting enough to keep in mind for a book called "So what I was *REALLY* thinking...."

I would like to thank my mother Roswitha McIntosh who provided countless hours of editing to simplify my writing. In addition to all the practical help toward book publishing, she is an inspiration to me and many others in her enthusiasm, intelligence and ability to take on any task or challenge with grace and determination.

I would like to thank my husband Craig whose support and love are all-encompassing. His facility with words has been crucial in clarifying meaning and improving readability. More importantly, with loving encouragement, he has always supported my endeavors, including my passion for continued education and waterskiing.

INTRODUCTION

Will a relationship become life-enhancing and fulfilling, or will it deteriorate into frustration and pain to the point where it ultimately fails?

The answer lies in the way you think about your relationships and communicate your needs, desires, and opinions. Whether or not a relationship thrives hinges on the quality of the countless interactions that occur between two people.

Think about the tone of voice, choice of words, and body language you use throughout the day. Do you nod in feigned agreement? Do you roll your eyes with contempt? Communicating disrespect through posture, sarcasm or condescension erodes the connection between people — the very foundation of a relationship. The quality of those innumerable ephemeral moments makes the difference between a fulfilling relationship and one fraught with disappointment and grief.

Similarly, your sense of self and wellbeing are formed by the totality of your thoughts and actions, and especially your inner dialogue. How you speak to yourself has enormous impact on your self-esteem, your enjoyment of life, and your effect on the people around you.

So... what I *REALLY* meant...

This book is a collection of over 200 examples of how you can transform common yet ineffective thoughts and statements into effective and productive communication. Often you simply need to reorient your thinking and rework the way you express yourself. Each example includes a brief psychological explanation and illustrates the skills needed to communicate successfully.

When you recognize your personal tendencies and relationship patterns before they lead to difficulties, you can avoid unnecessary pain and frustration. People who do *not* question themselves or examine their relationships risk getting blind-sided by the unexpected, such as the unforeseen affair, children with addictions, or the onset of financial problems.

When you broaden your perspective and fine-tune your communication skills, you can transform your life and improve the quality of your relationships.

Self-Empowerment

Enhanced self-awareness and understanding of your specific relationship dynamics allow you to live a more fulfilling life. By recognizing how you may be participating in certain relationship patterns, you can then exercise the primary power you have in your relationships — namely to decide how you will respond.

Mutual Respect and Self-respect

Mutual respect and self-respect create the fundamental basis of a healthy relationship. Mutual respect involves respecting the needs of others while valuing and taking care of your own needs and desires in a positive way.

Dealing with Anxiety

All intimate relationships involve some stress, anxiety, disagreement, and fear of loss. Thus, intimacy requires the ability to handle anxiety without being reactive — that is, without withdrawing suddenly, lashing out, or falling apart. Calmly withstanding the tension of anxiety and stress is crucial in sustaining good relationships and pursuing goals of any kind.

Moderating The Inner Critic

The inner critic that we all have can be encouraging and supportive or oppressive and degrading. Only when you learn to recognize and change the way you undermine yourself, can you recognize and prevent damaging behavior from others. In order to stop putting up with negative, judgmental, or destructive behavior from others, you must become understand and learn to transform your own inner critic and your own behavior.

Communication Skills

We all have thoughts and desires that sometimes need to be expressed to others. Do we communicate our thoughts and desires effectively? Are we communicating them at all? Poor communication and lack of communication lead to frustration and disappointment. Much of the emotional heat that wreaks havoc in relationships can be avoided when we fine-tune our choice of words, body language, tone of voice, and demeanor.

Avoiding Hostility and Control

Negative patterns between people often develop so gradually that it's hard to notice the disintegration of a relationship until it's too late. Conscious awareness of your own and others' boundaries can help you avoid descending into demeaning, hostile, or controlling relationships.

The Unconscious

Often the unconscious expresses itself through a defense mechanism that may have served a person well in the past, but becomes a limitation to living life fully. By examining expressions of your unconscious, such as attractions, dreams, outbursts, and recurrent relationship patterns, you can discover unconscious forces that move you. You can become more self-empowered, creative, and loving by recognizing and appreciating your unconscious vulnerabilities and drives. Through awareness, you can avoid letting your unconscious demons get the better of you, which allows you to live more consciously and intentionally.

Developing New Parts of Yourself

An individual's personality has a multitude of parts. We can be responsible, fun-loving, productive, fearful, or assertive, for example. Each part is a specific personality structure with its own history and way of being in the world. Sometimes particular parts of the personality take over while other parts get repressed, creating an unhealthy imbalance.

Becoming aware of how these primary parts of your personality are triggered and interact in the world gives you the ability to check and transform your automatic responses. It also gives you the opportunity to develop the undeveloped parts in a gradual, positive way, which allows for greater fulfillment. As a result, you can live a more multifaceted life and incorporate more depth and breadth into your relationships.

Influences

My psychological view of people and relationships has been modeled in large part on the theories of Carl Jung, particularly his theory of *individuation*, as well as Hal and Sidra Stone's *psychology of the selves*. Both Jung and the Stones emphasize the role of the unconscious that underlies the powerful dynamics that lead to *complexes* or different *selves* influencing an individual's behavior and triggering distress. Other influential notions include the theory of *differentiation* developed by Murray Bowen, and further applied by David Schnarch to sexual intimacy. Marshall Rosenberg's *nonviolent communication* provides an excellent framework for effective communication that is applied throughout this book. Exciting new findings in brain neuro-plasticity reveal ways that you can transform ineffective habits that keep you stuck, allowing you to have successful relationships and live the life that you desire.

SO... WHAT I *REALLY* MEANT...

1. COMMUNICATION

"That's wrong. I totally disagree!"

So what I really meant was...

"What leads you to that conclusion? Could you explain it to me?"

Or "What if we looked at it a little differently..."

It is the mark of an educated mind to be able to entertain a thought without accepting it.

~Aristotle

"Oh no! I'm trapped. She's gossiping again."

A little gossip may be healthy when its purpose is to spread good news, to gain insight, to have a harmless laugh or to protect a friend from harm. However, when spreading rumors only serves to get attention or malign someone, it brings everyone down. It also reveals to others that the perpetrator of gossip is not comfortable in his or her own skin and will strive to be the center of attention even at the cost of disparaging others.

When you feel yourself being lured into malicious gossip, spurring the perpetrator on with curiosity can end up making you feel uncharitable and mean-spirited afterwards. Here are some alternative ways to handle the conversation:

1. Change the Subject: "How's your work going?" Redirecting the conversation is the easiest way to handle gossip.
2. Devil's Advocate: "Let's take a look at it from Sarah's side." People who gossip are used to getting others' attention and agreement. They might be taken aback and stop gossiping if you defend the person being slandered.
3. Innuendo: "Let's talk about something more positive and decide what we're going to do this afternoon." This statement implies disapproval but is softened by changing the topic of discussion.
4. Direct: "I feel uncomfortable/uninspired/bored listening to gossip." This is direct and can be said to people who can handle honest criticism, or those whose gossip is particularly malicious.

"She says I frown all the time. That's just me."

What comes first, attitude or facial expression?

Your tone of voice, facial expressions, and words reflect your attitude about yourself, the person you're talking to, and life in general.

Brain research shows that changing your facial expression actually makes you feel different — smiling makes you feel happier, frowning makes you feel angrier, gestures like sighing make you feel more hopeless.

Not only do your feelings affect your facial expressions, but *your facial expressions affect how you feel — even if you fake them.*

Smile to feel happier

Research shows that if you watch a movie while holding a pen in your teeth across your mouth, which causes you to engage some of your smile muscles, you will think the movie is funnier than if you watched the movie without the pen. Simply smiling — even artificially — releases chemicals in the brain that make you feel happier. Try it.

I'm not advocating walking around with a fake smile on your face. But it is illuminating to see what impact your facial expressions have on your own mood and others. Becoming aware of whether you are scowling, grimacing, or sneering will allow you to choose to change your facial expressions, and to change the way you feel and others respond to you.

"Can't you see that I'm busy!"

So what I really meant was...

"I'd love to talk to you. Just give me 15 minutes to finish this project/write this letter/make a phone call."

Or "I just have a minute. What's on your mind?"

Or "I'm sorry, today is not a good day."

Over-generalizing: "You never show appreciation."

Seeing patterns and generalizing from them are crucial human skills. Scientists, business owners, and capable people in general develop the ability to spot patterns in human behavior.

Sweeping generalizations

Yet sometimes we make sweeping generalizations that exaggerate or oversimplify reality. When we take one unfortunate incident and jump to conclusions, we can create problems and offend people.

Over-generalizing is generally not helpful. People get defensive when you say things like the following:

- "You *never* show appreciation."
- "You spend *all* your time with your friends instead of with me."
- "You *always* interrupt me."

Limit focus to one event

It's more effective to be specific and talk about one incident at a time — the incident of the moment. Limit yourself to specific facts, and focus instead on a desired outcome. For instance,

- If you seek appreciation, you can ask, "Isn't this dinner I cooked delicious?"
- Instead of complaining about someone's frequent absence, you could suggest, "I'd like to spend some time with you. When can we get together?"
- To get someone to stop interrupting, you could say, "Please let me finish" each time you're interrupted.

Specific positive requests are more likely to get you what you want than gross generalizations.

"If I needed your advice, I'd ask for it!"

So what I really meant was…

"I appreciate your wanting to help, but… right now I have a strategy,"

Or "What I need right now is some time to reflect,"
Or "I'm sorry, but now is not a good time."

It takes a great man to give sound advice tactfully, but a greater man to accept it graciously."

~Macaulay, J. C.

Intrusive questions at family gatherings: "It's none of your business!"

Questions about when you'll finally get married, when you'll get a *real* job, or how the divorce is going may cause you to dread family gatherings. It's helpful to keep in mind that many relatives are truly concerned and simply want what's best for you, but they come off seeming overly nosey. Some might simply be trying to be considerate and to make conversation rather than intrude, while others may have more malicious intent.

Here are some ways to handle questions you'd rather avoid answering:

Divert

Steer the conversation in the direction of their lives: "Aw, that's not so interesting. What's going on in your life? How's your marriage going?" Or redirect with your own uncomfortable question, "First tell me how your sex life is going."

Try the quizzical eyebrow with a smile that says, "Can't you think of anything else to talk about? Come on now."

Use humor

If you show that you feel uncomfortable or upset, you simply draw attention to yourself and to the specific topic. Humor is a great way to deflect prying questions. If asked about something awkward, keep a positive, light-hearted attitude.

For instance, if someone asks about your divorce status or financial situation, try to be witty:

> "Every time I find Mr. Right, my husband scares him away."

> Or "Love is grand; divorce is a hundred grand."

> ~Shinichi Suzuki

Be up front

If you know that someone is going to ask you when you are finally going to have children or some other unwelcome question, you might approach that person first in private, and say something like, "I know you want us to have children, but we haven't made that decision yet. Let's not bring it up at dinner." Try not to get upset or defensive; that only peaks other people's curiosity.

Avoid

As a last resort, if you can't handle tasteless, mean-spirited questions, avoid them all together by avoiding the people who insist on asking them.

"We never go dancing or do anything fun anymore!"

So what I really meant was…
"Let's go dancing!"

Self-pity is unattractive. Exaggeration and blame put people on the defensive. Playing the victim is definitely not a seductive way to get someone to want to go dancing with you!

When people show excitement and personal authority they have a lot more magnetism than when they complain. Focus on the underlying desire, which is to go dancing. So say it in a positive, irresistible way: "I'd love it if you came dancing with me tonight/next week/every Saturday!"

"I feel overwhelmed thinking about my family visiting next week."

When facing a family visit, people often have ambivalent feelings, wanting to make everyone happy, yet dreading the work and potential personal conflicts that loom ahead.

Expectations

You may feel obligated to put everyone up at your house and prepare all the meals because you think that's what is expected of you. While giving to others can be deeply fulfilling, it's best to give at a level where you can do so wholeheartedly and lovingly rather than resentfully. You don't want to slip into martyrdom.

Instead of succumbing to what you think is expected, decide what you are willing to do and state so up front.

If, for example, you are happy to prepare one meal, graciously invite everyone for that meal. "I invite you all for dinner on Friday night. On Saturday, we can go out," or "You're on your own." "You can pick up your favorite breakfast groceries at the store down the street."

People like to know what is expected in the way of itinerary, sleeping arrangements, kids' rules, differing holiday traditions, and dogs. If you clarify expectations and don't promise too much, you can be giving without becoming exasperated and resentful. When you communicate clearly ahead of time, people are less likely to be disappointed because they understand the game plan and your expectations.

Saying "No."

If your relatives or friends tend to ignore your requests, hints, and desires, or are generally unpleasant, then there's no need to accommodate them with meals or housing, unless you are willing and able to live up to Mother Theresa's philosophy: *People are generally irrational, unreasonable and selfish. Love them anyway.*

You can say "no" while still communicating warm-heartedly. For example, "That's not a good weekend for us to have visitors. We would love to see you though if you come into town. Call us and we'll meet for coffee/a drink/lunch."

Stonewalling: "I don't have the time to deal with this right now."

Stonewalling is a technique used by people to deliberately delay having to respond or cooperate with others. A stonewaller stalls or refuses to make a decision, have a discussion, or listen to another point of view.

Discussions and joint decision-making are essential parts of a relationship. In many cases, other people may need an answer:

- "My parents invited us for Thanksgiving; should we go?"
- "I'd like to get that home entertainment center."

- "I received a great job offer outside of Stonewall City. Are willing to move?"

Occasionally, stonewalling within reason can be a way of taking the time needed to contemplate a difficult situation. However, if stonewalling becomes commonplace whenever a difficult question arises, problems will worsen causing relationships to disintegrate into isolation and resentment.

If you need time to consider something, say so.

Nothing is more important in a relationship than the ability to openly discuss differences of opinion and preferences. So if you tend to stonewall, it's essential that you learn to make some response right away even if it is just to buy yourself time. At least suggest a specific time or day when you'll discuss the situation in question, and then follow-through.

Dealing with a stonewaller

If you are dealing with a stonewaller, ask for specific detail and a time-frame. To ease communication, you can say, "I'd like to know what you'd prefer to do or what your pros and cons are regarding this decision."

A stonewaller is often afraid of conflict or is uncomfortable expressing his or her feelings and preferences. So, it's important to be compassionate and avoid being reactive when he or she *does* communicate.

"Stop nagging me about watching the game!"

So what I really meant was...

"Please don't ask me to give up something that I really enjoy. I'd like to watch the game without feeling guilty about it."

While *some* sacrifices need to be made in any relationship, giving up what you truly enjoy for the sake of the relationship will only lead to resentment — not to love and appreciation. Support your partner's passions and expect reciprocity.

However, make sure that you do spend quality time with your partner on a regular basis even if you feel like Arnold Mendel about football:

> *Football is not a game but a religion, a metaphysical island of fundamental truth in a highly verbalized, disguised society, a throwback of 30,000 generations of anthropological time.*

> ~Arnold Mendel

"No one ever helps me with the dishes!"

Try a constructive and positive approach, "It would be great if you could help with the dishes." People generally like to help, *if* they feel they will be appreciated for helping, but *not* if guilt is used to get them to help. Guilt is a poor motivator. If your request doesn't work, then add, "I really need your help right now. Please help me do the dishes." Sound friendly but firm in your resolve.

If getting your family to help is a daily problem, plan ahead and ask, "Who wants to chop vegetables and set the table, and who wants to wash the dishes?"

If none of these work because your family dynamics are too entrenched, you may think about buying paper plates or going out to eat on your own. Just say, "I'm pretty overwhelmed with work and will treat myself to no dishes. You're on your own tonight." Go on strike in a positive way — that will get their attention.

Sarcasm: *"Carry it yourself! Your arms aren't broken."*

Not so funny

Sarcastic people often hide behind an excuse such as, "I was just being funny" or "I was only kidding." While humor makes people laugh, sarcasm typically does not.

The word comes from the Greek *sarkasmos* meaning "to tear flesh, gnash the teeth, and speak bitterly." Sarcasm signifies "the use of irony, to mock, or to convey contempt." An attitude of contempt communicates the belief that you are unworthy of respect. It's no longer funny when you're being treated as though you are unworthy of respect.

People use sarcasm when they cannot be direct

People often use sarcasm because they have been treated poorly themselves, which creates a desire to retaliate by making other people feel foolish. Thus, the miserable cycle of using biting cynicism in interaction with others fuels itself.

Sarcasm is a defense mechanism used by people who may have been taught to feel uncomfortable talking about such unmanly things as feelings, needs and desires — e.g., being tired, overwhelmed, sad, angry, or needing help. They expect or hope that others will know what they feel and need.

Ironically, when we avoid expressing our needs or vulnerabilities, it can lead to a subversive upwelling of those vulnerabilities, which in turn can manifest itself in sarcasm. When you cannot express yourself in a straightforward manner, issues may simmer below the surface and may erupt in a hurtful, sarcastic way.

Be direct

Instead of saying "Are your arms broken?" it's much more effective to state why you don't want to carry something or otherwise undertake the task at hand. Here are some ideas of what you could say without attacking the other person:

- "Sorry, I'm too tired. I've worked a lot today,"
- "I've got my hands full."
- "I think you can handle it."
- "I would appreciate it if you would do it."
- "I'm exhausted. Right now I need to relax."

Can't take a Compliment: "It was nothing; anyone could have done it."

If you feel uncomfortable when receiving a compliment, consider the feelings of the people giving the compliment. They are often simply attempting to make you feel good, and like to be acknowledged for their effort.

Certainly some compliments are more meaningful than others. Some are specific, genuine, and address something you have made an effort to accomplish. Others are less meaningful, because they are general, manipulative, or address a quality that you were born with, such as having nice eyes.

In either case, there's generally no reason to be dismissive of a compliment. Even if the compliment is given in an attempt to manipulate you, graciously accepting it doesn't mean you'll let it influence your actions.

Some people fear that they will come across as arrogant if they accept a compliment too readily. Taking in a compliment does *not* mean letting it go to your head. A person's self-worth is rarely based on what others think. Yet it is enjoyable to soak in kind words like a few rays of sunshine.

Taking a moment to feel gratitude when you are treated well is also a gift for the person giving the compliment. People enjoy knowing they have made you feel good. Letting your appreciation show with a smile or a "Thank you," or "That means a lot to me," also encourages them to continue to look for the good in people.

Too often we underestimate the power of a touch, a smile, a kind word, a listening ear, an honest compliment, or the smallest act of caring, all of which have the potential to turn a life around.

~Leo F. Buscaglia

Shame: "What's wrong with you? You are good for nothing!"

The pain of shame

Someone who feels deep shame is consumed by feelings of despair for being flawed and unworthy. Too much shame is difficult to bear, and can lead to self-destructive behavior, addiction, depression, and in some cases, suicide.

Shame leads to self-sabotaging behavior

Even when people who feel deep shame are doing well, they expect others to be disappointed in them. Their shame often leads to self-sabotaging behavior, which causes them to get the response they feel they deserve. Their failures promote the type of attention they are used to receiving.

Thus, it can be difficult and heartbreaking to deal with people whose reckless behavior is caused by their belief that they don't deserve any better. We often want to motivate them to change by pointing out how flawed and mistaken their behavior and actions are. In such situations, however, any kind of criticism may encourage low self-esteem and more self-destructive behavior.

What if someone does something wrong?

While it *is* important to set boundaries, enforce consequences, communicate our disappointment, and protect ourselves, it is *not* necessary to shame and humiliate another person. While harmful behavior *should* be met with repercussions, we have to be careful that our good intentions do not get expressed as contempt for the other person.

Communication without judgment

Expressing your feelings about someone's behavior and setting boundaries are fundamentally different from judging a person as worthless, as in the following denunciation: "What is wrong with you — you good for nothing!"

Communication should be factual rather than judgmental: "When you did such and such, I was disappointed and angry. I'm asking you to…. As a result, I will no longer…."

People who have been deeply shamed need to be loved, valued, and spoken to honestly rather than judged, while still being held accountable for their actions. Often a therapist can help them stop their negative self-criticism and restore in them a feeling of self-worth.

"We never do anything romantic anymore!"

So what I really meant was…
to quote Billy Crystal,
"You look MAAAHvelous! Let's go to dinner, the movies, or on a walk under the stars tonight."

Giving Advice: "She never listens to me!"

Advice is like snow; the softer it falls, the longer it dwells upon, and the deeper it sinks into the mind.

~Samuel Taylor Coleridge

There may be a compelling reason why someone doesn't appear to be listening to you. It may be your timing, tone of voice, wording, or tendency to repeat yourself. It may be the fact that the person is not interested in getting advice. Here are some parameters to consider when giving advice:

1. Select an appropriate time and private setting to talk.
2. Find out the person's state of mind or point of view to make sure your advice is appropriate.
3. Ask the person whether she would like some advice. Or ask if you could tell a personal story that might have some bearing on the situation.
4. Frame your advice as a positive suggestion rather than negative criticism.
5. Remember that no one knows for sure what is best for another person.
6. Don't repeat advice. Pushiness has a negative effect; it builds resistance.
7. Respect the other person's autonomy. Let him or her decide whether or not to take your advice.

The true secret of giving advice is, after you have honestly given it, to be perfectly indifferent whether it is taken or not, and never persist in trying to set people right.

~Hannah Whitall Smith

"I can do it myself!! Leave me alone!"

So what I really meant was…

"No thank you. I'll do it myself."

An irritated, angry tone of voice broadcasts emotional dependence while a polite, decisive tone of voice reveals emotional independence.

Flattery: "Meet my friend, the CEO and triathlete with a house in the Hamptons."

When you introduce friends in a social setting by flattering them, you probably just want to make them feel good. But here are some unintended negative consequences of flattery:

1. You create expectations. You don't let your friend establish his or her own impression and identity. You taint the new relationship with preconceived notions rather than allowing a rapport to evolve in a more interesting and natural way.

2. You reduce friends to their résumés. You imply that you primarily appreciate your friends for their achievements and may not appreciate the nuance and mystery of who they really are.

3. You ignore the subtleties. The character and intangible essence of a person are more important than a checklist of accomplishments.

4. You use your friend to enhance your status. You give the impression that you are trying to boost your own self-esteem by boasting about being connected to someone "important," "smart," or "talented." This

often reveals a desire to compensate for feelings of inadequacy.

5. You embarrass your friend. Blatant flattery puts friends on the defensive and in the position of being embarrassed. They may then feel they have to downplay their accomplishments or alternatively to make sure they live up to them.

6. You cause others to feel inferior. By playing up your friend's achievements, you might cause others to feel inadequate.

There are some people who will be delighted if you introduce them with a fanfare-accompanied list of their achievements. However, you actually show more faith in a friend by introducing him or her with a simple "This is my friend Alex."

Of course, there are always exceptions. In business, relevant detailed introductions are necessary, and sometimes it is helpful to let people know that they have something of interest in common. Both can be done without flattery.

> *Nothing is so great an example of bad manners as flattery. If you flatter all the company, you please none; If you flatter only one or two, you offend the rest.*
>
> ~Jonathan Swift

"You NEVER compliment me!"

So what I really meant was...

"Hey, I'd love for you to give me a compliment once in a while! Make it good, and I'll reciprocate."

It's hard to resist a flatterer who gets it right.

~Robert Brault

"I never call my mom and dad because we have nothing to talk about."

Connection

When you call a relative, it doesn't matter that you don't have much to talk about. Making a call shows that you care. Simply calling to make a connection is what counts.

There is no need to have long conversations or bring up topics that will generate conflict, unless there is something specific that you want to resolve. Asking how they are doing or even talking about the weather does the job of making a connection.

Awkward questions

If you're afraid your parent will ask awkward questions, such as "Are you still seeing what's-her-name — you know the girl with the purple hair?" there's no need to respond reactively. Look for the positive concern underlying the question, even if there's more sarcasm than concern. "Amy, yes, we're doing great, thank you."

If they ask when you're finally going to get a real job, take the high road with your response by saying for example, "I appreciate your concern. I'm glad to have any job right now. Please don't worry about my finances. I'm doing fine."

If a parent is particularly critical, say calmly, "Hi, I called you to say *hello*. Tell me what's going on. Anything good?" Then switch the subject or get off the phone. "Have a great week. I'll talk to you again soon."

The longer a person goes without calling a particular person, the more resistance he or she will feel about doing it. Keeping these connections alive can mean a lot for everyone involved over the long-term, and can be particularly meaningful for parents as they age. One day you'll be glad to hear your children on the phone asking, "How are you doing, Mom and Dad?"

However, if your parent has been abusive, it may be best for your wellbeing to direct your efforts toward non-family members who appreciate and reciprocate your time and kindness.

Inspiring vs. Pushing: "Why don't you just believe in yourself!!"

When we care for others, we often want to push them to improve their lives and pursue lofty goals. We want the best for them. Sometimes the problem is that *we* believe in them more than *they* believe in themselves. So we try to push them to become what we see in them. Our intentions are noble, our passion is authentic, but our actions may create resistance.

Pushing can backfire

The trouble is that people are likely to perceive your excessive urging as a manifestation of your disappointment — and to some degree it is. They usually will not respond with "Yes, you're right. I *can* do this." Instead they may be thinking, "I'm never good enough. Everyone is disappointed in me again."

Being pushy, even with the best intentions, also minimizes the importance of autonomy and the need for inner motivation. Thus, excessive prodding will often trigger resistance.

Encourage through listening

Encouraging words are more likely to be taken in and believed when they are spoken earnestly but without excessive force. It's fine to say, "I know you can do it." However, it's best to avoid bringing heat, exaggeration, and repetition to that encouragement. That which proves too much, proves nothing.

As Dean Rusk said, "One of the best ways to persuade others is with your ears — by listening." Effective persuasion starts by allowing the other person to discover his or her underlying motivations. Unfortunately, you cannot "motivate" a person who does not have an inkling of self-motivation. The best inspiration, thus, comes from example, true friendship, and allowing others to make their own mistakes.

> *Far better to live your own path imperfectly than to live another's perfectly.*
>
> ~Bhagavad Gita

"You are such a jerk, calling me names like that!"

It's important not to accept named-calling or abuse in any situation. It is just as important to avoid participating in verbal attacks and abuse toward others. While there is a place for serious anger, it's rarely effective to attack the verbally abusive person to defend yourself. If you cannot prevent yourself from attacking the other person, put off the conversation.

"I can't discuss this right now. I'm too angry."

When a friend has lost a loved one: "I haven't called yet because I don't know what to say."

When a person experiences a tragedy like the loss of a child or partner, that loss will remain at the forefront of his or her mind for a very long time.

People differ in how they like to be approached about such a loss. Most people prefer that others acknowledge their loss in some manner — either through direct contact or a written note of condolence.

While eventually the loss will feel less painful, life will never be the same after losing a child or partner. People who have lost a loved one need to grieve. It's not helpful to point out that their pain may diminish. The idea of feeling better may seem like a betrayal of their love for the person they loved and lost.

Nothing you say will eliminate the pain. The most meaningful thing you can do is to reach out and acknowledge their loss and to remember the life of their loved one. You can also ask what you can do to help, such as bringing a meal or going to the store. You can express your compassion by simply being present or giving a hug without a word.

Most importantly, don't avoid talking about and helping celebrate the loved one's life. People whom we remember stay alive within us. Those who care most won't turn away, but they will keep the memory, the love, and the person alive, even while life inevitably moves on.

In memory of Dex Gannon and Michael Young

"I've been standing here for 25 minutes!! What took you so long?"

So what I really meant was...

"I'm glad you're here, I was worried something might have happened to you."

Before accusing someone of wrongdoing, it's best to find out what happened. If someone has a reasonable excuse, you will feel foolish if you get angry without hearing the explanation first.

If waiting for the same person becomes a repeated occurrence, then it's time to stop depending on that person. Either leave after 15 minutes or meet in a place where you don't mind waiting because you're busy doing other things.

"My wife seems obsessed with criticizing an acquaintance."

While your wife's preoccupation *seems* to be about the acquaintance, it's probably more about herself. When people are fascinated or obsessed by another person or their flaws, there is probably something deeper going on and worthwhile looking into if they are willing to be reflective.

Without putting your wife on the defensive, you may want to point out how focused she seems to be on that particular person's flaws. You could say, "I notice that you talk about Ella a lot. I'm curious why she interests you so much? Does anything about her situation worry you or remind you of something going on in your own life?"

If she doesn't know, here are some ideas you might suggest in a diplomatic way.

- She may feel rejected by the acquaintance.
- She may be feeling jealous.
- She may dislike her for possessing a specific trait that she lacks in herself.

For example, the acquaintance might be open, gregarious, and free, while your wife is shy, quiet and conservative. A fascination of this kind is sometimes caused by an unconscious yearning to develop the very qualities that a person finds bothersome in the other person. She simply finds it easier to malign the other person than to try to develop those qualities in moderation in herself.

While some people embody particular qualities in the extreme — making them appear distasteful — integrating a small dose of any quality gives you more flexibility to respond to and embrace the myriad circumstances we encounter in life.

Telemarketing: "How would you like it if I called you at home during dinner!?"

So what I really meant was...

"Please put me on your do-not-call list. We don't want to receive marketing calls. Have a good evening." Then hang up. Click.

Firmly but politely request to be taken off the marketing list, and remember, telemarketers are just people doing their job, which is not always a pleasant one.

Drunk Driving: "I hate driving with you when you've been drinking too much!"

If your partner or friend has been drinking too much and insists on driving with you on board, notice your reaction. Do you hesitate because you're afraid of upsetting him or her and then comply?

The dangerous desire to comply

When you're not aware of the psychological forces that motivate you, they can wreak havoc in your life. This is a situation where the desire to comply in order to get along can endanger your life and the lives of others. You have an obligation to yourself and others to act.

Accommodating others is reasonable as long as there's no harm at stake and you are not simply motivated to avoid the anxiety associated with non-compliance. Beware of acquiescing to pressure when it compromises your own safety and wellbeing. It is not worth temporarily appeasing an out-of-control or inebriated person. Nor does it show respect for yourself or others.

Be brave

It's vital to be able to withstand the dread of standing up against forceful demands from others. When an intoxicated person pressures you with "I'm fine; just get in the car," you don't need to convince him or her of anything. You don't need to argue. In fact, arguing with someone who is drunk can also be dangerous. Walk away, be safe and, if appropriate, notify the authorities.

If the person is really drunk and could endanger others on the road, it takes additional courage to take away the keys or call the police. Not only could you save someone else's life, but you may save the drunk driver's life as well. It's better for the intoxicated person to go to jail and experience embarrassment and anger than to live with the consequences of having injured or killed someone.

"Stop wolfing down your food!"

So what I really meant was...
"We have time. Let's enjoy this wonderful meal!"

"I'm shocked at how much I criticize my Dad for letting people walk all over him and for not standing up for himself."

Always a disappointment

I suspect your dad's behavior stems from a deep belief that he is not worthy of being cared for and loved. Feelings of inadequacy often result when people never received real affection or acknowledgement from their own parents. People who consider themselves to have "disappointed" their parents often set themselves up to perpetuate the cycle of being a disappointment to others.

Heated encouragement vs. criticism

I'm sure the intention behind your criticism is that your dad become more self-empowered. If you are feeling critical, you are probably using too much passion when you encourage him to have faith in himself. Passionate encouragement can be taken the wrong way. The words are meant to be convincing and uplifting: "You deserve better! Stop letting people walk all over you!"

Yet the vigorous tone of your remark may be heard by him as further proof that he is always disappointing others including you. He probably hears your encouragement as, "You're never good enough." The message he hears further reinforces his feelings of inadequacy.

Acceptance

Often the most compelling thing we can do, particularly with adult relatives, is to accept them, warts and all, without trying to change them. Being kind and having a sense of humor — not the mean sarcastic type — are wonderful ways of showing love and acceptance.

"No, don't bring John to my party. He's loud and obnoxious."

If a friend wants to bring someone to your party whom you don't care for, you *don't* have to say "yes." If you are going to feel resentful about having that person at your house, that's a sign that you *should* say "no."

There's no reason to be negative and judgmental though. That would simply put your friend on the defensive.

Keep it positive and limit yourself to "I" statements: "I just want to have close friends at my party. I'd really like you to come, but I'm not that close to John. Sorry to disappoint you." Or, "There are a lot of people coming already. I'd rather not invite anyone else. Sorry. But I hope *you* can make it."

Being upbeat, light-hearted, and guilt-free is best!

"I can't stand it when people talk over me."

Interrupt cordially

When you deal with someone who interrupts you a lot, you need to learn how to keep talking anyway, without being angry, sullen, or hurt. Or you can say, "Please wait! Let me finish," and then continue with your story.

There's no need to give an evil glare and announce, "You're interrupting me again!" That makes the other person feel like a scolded child and view you as a critical parent — a dynamic that leads to hurt and embarrassment.

Instead, interrupt back in a passionate way, showing that you're excited about what you're saying. Also, be sure to give the other person an opportunity to speak when you are finished.

Customs and people differ

People differ greatly in how comfortable they are interrupting in order to get a word into a conversation. In Italy, you will never be heard unless you're willing to jump in and *make* yourself be heard because it is likely that several people will be talking simultaneously. People who have been raised in quieter, more reserved environments can benefit from learning to assert themselves around enthusiastic conversationalists.

On the other hand, passionate interrupters might benefit by exercising their patience and listening skills. But you'll need to interrupt assertively to suggest something like that to them.

"What's with your hair? You look ridiculous!"

So what I really meant was...

27

"Interesting hairdo."

Tend to your own feelings of embarrassment over the appearance of friends and family members, rather than worry how it might reflect poorly on you.

If someone asks for your opinion, that's a different story. Or if you know the person is open to your opinion, go ahead and give advice, "I like it better when you comb your hair." "I prefer you with brown hair over green." But usually it's best to allow others the autonomy to experiment with harmless expressions of their individuality.

You may want to make an exception and make your opinion known when you take someone to a more formal event where wild hair and attire would be insulting to your hosts.

"You sound like a broken record complaining about your psycho ex!"

Focusing on the ex

People often remain stuck in a state of anger when they can't get past the wrong that's been done to them, be it real or perceived. Some painful pattern in the past keeps them reviewing past events *ad nauseam*. They yearn for justice but can't get the relief they want because they are not dealing with the real hurt underlying the situation. Focusing on the ex is a way of avoiding the real challenge, which is to look within oneself.

People fixated on their exes often fear that they are somehow inadequate or unlovable. For instance, being married without feeling appreciated can leave a person feeling undeserving of love or recognition. Only when a person starts recognizing and resolving his or her own hidden vulnerability is there a chance of dealing effectively with what really matters. That's when the process of healing and growth can begin.

Responding in a helpful way

As a friend, it's not healthy to pile on with negative judgments about the culprit involved. The best thing you can do is to point out the harmful pattern that you're concerned about. Also, listen for what's behind the obsessive anger — it's usually an underlying vulnerability or fear.

Depending on the underlying issue, you might say something like, "It seems that you did not get much appreciation. I wonder how you could avoid seeking appreciation from people who don't or can't give it?" Ask how they think they can best deal with the underlying need, without repeatedly going over how they've been hurt. Ask how they might best focus on recognizing and appreciating their own self-worth. Remind them that self-worth blossoms when you focus on pursuing passions, helping and engaging others, and living life fully.

Explain to your friend how detrimental it is when we rehash stories of being a victim, because it prevents us from making positive changes. It is far better to take note of the lesson we have learned and use it to improve our future.

Getting off the phone: "I can never get off the phone with certain people who like to talk a lot."

It can be hard to get off the phone with big talkers because you don't want to hurt their feelings and you don't want to interrupt them. But remember, *your* time is valuable too! While you don't need to hurt anyone's feelings, you may *have* to interrupt. If you're not using caller ID and you get hooked in, simply break into the conversation and say, one of the following:

- *Let's talk when I'm off work.*
- *I just have a minute. What's on your mind?*
- *Can we talk on Tuesday?*
- *I'll have a little time after finishing this project/feeding the kids/tomorrow.*
- *Let's talk after next week.*

When you're able to get off the phone quickly, easily and politely, then you won't dread it when you hear the phone ring. If some people still don't understand that you have different priorities and that your time is valuable, then you can't worry too much about offending them. They need to get the message that you are not available for ongoing conversation, venting, and chitchat.

If you allow yourself to get hooked in on a repeated basis, your friend will get the message that you *are* available as a sympathetic ear. Simply interject, *I'm sorry, but I've got a lot of work to do. Take care. Have a great day.* And hang up — CLICK.

"He's such a caveman! Same old Disappointment on Valentine's Day."

Disappointment on Valentine's Day is a reminder to reflect on your fantasies and your expectations of others. The media's extravagant marketing and fantastic movie moments create unrealistic expectations for both men and women. There's no way to live up to those cinematic romantic moments, at least not without set decorators and a film crew. They express dramatic and unrealistic fiction.

You are never going to be in a relationship with someone who is totally tuned with your desires unless you communicate those desires clearly. Moreover, you would lose your desire for someone who spent all his or her time trying to read your mind and then satisfy your every fantasy.

No single person has it all. Individuals whose declaration of their unrequited love is emblazoned on the side of the Goodyear blimp may be lacking in other desirable qualities. Those exciting types may end up sending exotic Brazilian flowers dripping with diamonds to someone else next year — to your surprise! So you might learn to appreciate your caveman for simply not staging the perfect date.

Life is too short to waste time wishing that your partner knew what your private fantasies are. Yet if your idea of what should happen on Valentine's Day or any day is important to you, instead of playing a guessing game, state clearly what your expectations are.

Suggest, "I'd love to be surprised one night by...." Or you can make your particular fantasy happen yourself, in your own way. If you can't fly off to Paris, then set the table with a checkered cloth and enjoy some wine at home. If you don't have a partner, you can still embrace romance and have fun with a relative or friend by creating and enjoying an evening of intimate ambiance together.

2. Self-empowerment

"What do you mean! I'm fine! I don't need psychology!"

You don't have to have problems to be able to improve your life and your relationships by gaining deeper psychological understanding. The more insight you gain into the human psyche the more fulfilling your life can become.

We're all human, which means we all have contradictory drives and motivations striving to get our attention. For example, we want to achieve, *and* we want to relax. We want to have fun, *and* we want to be responsible. We want to please others, *and* we want to follow our own heart.

Unconscious biases are at the root of many problems. When we make decisions based on unconscious motivations and biases, we are not truly exercising choice, but rather being driven by fears and desires that have taken on a power of their own. One-sided unconscious tendencies often lead to unexpected and painful situations, such as affairs, conflict, or financial problems.

For example, someone who has experienced a chaotic upbringing might become a perfectionist in the home. Driven to maintain a well-organized home, he or she might unknowingly become excessively critical of his or her partner. As a result, the criticized partner may begin to feel resentful and inadequate in the home and seek validation from outside the relationship, further weakening the primary relationship, and perhaps even leading to an affair. Ironically, in seeking to establish order without awareness of unconscious forces, the result may end up worsening the chaos.

By fully understanding how our underlying drives function, sometimes *for* and sometimes *against* our overall wellbeing, we can ascertain how we unconsciously favor certain motivations at the expense of others. By gaining insight into our patterns and triggers and by learning psychological tools, we can avoid self-sabotaging behavior, by becoming more objective, softening our one-sided drives, and exercising real power by *truly* having a choice. We can also be better prepared for the winds of change.

Relationship challenges and personal symptoms can be viewed as signals that require our attention in order to adjust our life's journey. When we embrace life's challenges as opportunities to gain psychological understanding, we can transform the way we think and communicate, which will improve our relationships and allow us to live more successfully the life we desire.

Seeking approval: "Why doesn't my father appreciate me and all that I have accomplished?"

The irony of craving approval

Some people crave approval while others may enjoy it but don't think about it much. Those who either did not receive enough approval or received unrealistic amounts of adulation while growing up are usually the ones craving it. Those who received adequate amounts of approval have generally internalized a sense of self-approval. Thus, they may like it but don't long for it.

The outside world mirrors our inner sense of self-approval. So sadly, those who seek it most are least likely to receive it, while those who feel good about themselves and thus don't crave approval receive it easily.

The paradox of seeking approval

In the presence of close family members we sometimes revert back to being a child. We may still crave the approval that we feel we never received.

The trouble with seeking approval is threefold:

1. The approval we seek may be sought from someone who is incapable of giving it.

2. The more we yearn for that outside approval, the less likely we are to receive it because people who are reluctant to give approval are negatively triggered by those who yearn for it.

3. By the time we are adults, the disapproval we sense has become internalized. Therefore, we have to generate the approval we seek within ourselves rather than seeking it from others.

Even if your father finally sees the light and says, "You are amazing! I'm so proud of you," you will probably not feel that magical feeling of self-worth you've desired for so long. By the time you're an adult, the feeling of inadequacy stems from your internalized father — that internal negative voice that has been with you so long.

Transforming the internal voice

Now it is up to you to transform the voice in your head. This may be as difficult as transforming your real father. However, it's a relief to know that you actually have considerable control over your own thinking.

Through repeated thought replacement, you can develop new habits of thinking and thereby eventually create that sought-after approval and inner harmony. You need to catch yourself every time you have a negative thought and replace it with a positive one.

For instance, when you hear an inner voice saying, "I'm probably going to botch my interview," replace it with, "I will prepare for this interview as well as I can and do my best." After fifty or a hundred thought replacements, each successive one becomes easier. After a few hundred or thousand replacements, your habit will have changed.

Or replace the thought, "I'm never good enough for him to appreciate me," with a more positive thought: "Too bad for him that he isn't able to show appreciation, but I know I did a good job." After many such replacements, more constructive thinking will come automatically and your craving for approval from the outside will diminish.

Changing your Victim Story: "My dad was an alcoholic and my mom was never there for me."

Our story, our persona

It seems to be human nature to explain our lives and those of others' in the framework of a story. Without realizing it, we take specific events from our childhood and create a story around them, and eventually understand that story as the whole truth.

However, our interpretation of what happened is partly a work of fiction because we view events through our own limited lens. Notice how siblings experience their parents and upbringings in vastly different ways.

Our childhood experiences can keep us stuck in the past or motivate us to aim for a better future. When we repeat the same stories to ourselves and others, we trap ourselves into being victims of our past. By living our past forward, we avoid taking responsibility for our future.

Healing fiction

Once we grow up, we have the choice to let go of the stories we cling to. Psychologist James Hillman suggests that the soul seeks fiction that heals, and that we should take our personal history *literarily* rather than *literally*. This means seeing the depth and mythological dimension of the underlying forces that move the people and actions in our story.

For example, rather than thinking of yourself as a victim of your parents' dysfunctions, you could think of yourself as someone who has found inner strength, unknown capabilities, and a desire to seek new dreams. You could view your experience of pain and hardship as the way in which you found those strengths and dreams you never knew you had. Think, for example, how Nelson Mandela viewed and treated his 27 year incarceration. He learned to take pride in accomplishing mundane tasks well in order to maintain his dignity.

Instead of locking yourself into the limits of your past, you can use your creative imagination to look at your life through a new prism. When you change the story about your past, you create an opportunity to direct your future. By becoming one who has successfully overcome past challenges, you invite inner strength and vitality and move toward finding your soul's purpose.

Resentment Part 1: The need for self-empowerment.
"She got the job even though I work much harder. Hard work is a waste of time."

Resentment is the feeling of bitterness or hatred resulting from a real or imagined wrong. The key difference between resentment, anger, and contempt stems from how a person perceives the status of the wrongdoer.

Resentment is directed at people with perceived higher status.

Anger is directed at people with perceived equal status.

Contempt is directed at people with perceived lower status.

Causes

Resentment is often triggered when a person feels humiliated or rejected by another person with real or imagined power. There is a feeling of being used, taken advantage of, or being unrecognized for achievements while others succeed without equal merit.

When people feel they have no power to address unfair or demeaning treatment, negative feelings become internalized. Resentful people gain an air of bitterness, which causes others to overlook or reject them even more. By dwelling on negative feelings, resentment intensifies the problem of being belittled and marginalized.

Thus, working on your personal authority and self-empowerment is key to eliminating feelings of resentment.

To enhance your own self-empowerment:

1. Recognize people who take advantage of you. Try to limit your exposure to them.

2 Learn to speak up for yourself in a positive way, without being defensive or petty.

3. Own your own achievements, avoiding the extremes of excessive humility and being a braggart.

Resentment Part 2: Insidious Discontent. "If I say anything, it will just make things worse."

Signs of Resentment

To recognize that you are feeling resentful, consider whether you've been behaving in any of the following ways:

- Using phony friendliness to cover your true feelings.
- Speaking sarcastically about the person resented.
- Speaking in a demeaning way about the person resented.
- Expressing agitation and unexpected anger for no apparent reason.

Effects of Resentment

People who live with resentment have a difficult time overcoming powerlessness. To protect themselves from disappointment, people who feel disempowered tend to lower their expectations of others. Over time, low expectations results in cynicism and hostility.

These negative attitudes protect a person by closing the heart. As a result, it becomes difficult to trust others and to experience love and intimacy in closer relationships. Thus, resentment is isolating and painful, particularly when it is felt toward someone close.

Are you allowing yourself to be treated unfairly?

A healthier way to deal with resentment is to figure out how you may have participated in letting someone treat you unfairly. Sometimes people have little or no choice in a given situation, as for example, being a child in an abusive family. But in many cases, people unwittingly allow situations to become unfair. Recognizing how you tend to allow people to treat you poorly enables you to choose to avoid repeating the same pattern.

Questions to ask yourself:

1. Is the unfair treatment real or imagined? If real, why did that person treat you badly?

2. Why do you hesitate to respond with more personal power? Are you afraid of conflict? Do you feel undeserving?

3. How is your lack of personal power hurting you more than if you faced possible disapproval or loss?

4. Are you afraid to speak up for yourself because you tend to become defensive and make things worse? How could you learn to speak up assertively — with a positive attitude?

5. How would your life improve if you were to eliminate the resentment you experience?

When people have the courage to speak up for themselves *without* any bitterness, they gain confidence and optimism. In turn, others are *much less* likely to treat them unfairly, and if they do, they no longer get away with it.

Resentment Part 3: Irrational thinking: "I'll reject them before they reject me."

Resentment eats away at a person's wellbeing. The resentful person becomes unhappy, works less effectively, and pushes people away. Ironically, the person resented is not called to task and is likely not affected by the resentment. Living with resentment, therefore, is one of the most *ineffective* ways to live your life.

Often resentment is based on irrational thoughts. So if we clear up our thinking, sometimes we can eliminate this bitter feeling and its ill effects.

Irrational thoughts and their alternatives:

1. *Speaking up for oneself is wrong or abrasive.*
    ~Reality: Not speaking up often causes more harm than good.

2. *There are no disagreements in good relationships.*
    ~Reality: On the contrary, when people hide their opinions and feelings to avoid conflict, such suppression can lead to resentment, which is not a recipe for good relationships! Disagreement, preferably diplomatic disagreement, is a necessary ingredient for a good relationship.

3. *I'm a victim; no one will accept me. So, I'll reject them before they reject me.*
    ~Reality: This is a self-fulfilling prophecy. People are more likely to be accepting of you if you have enough self-assurance to be accepting of others, warts and all.

4. *I'll never win at anything I try; I'm unlucky.*

~Reality: Successful people learn from mistakes and persevere through failure. The willingness to experience failure opens the door to success.

5. *It's who you know that matters.*

    ~Reality: Many people work their way to happiness and success through hard work, learning from their mistakes, and maintaining a good attitude. While knowing the right person does help you get a foot in the door, it does not keep you in the room.

It's important to identify situations that trigger your irrational thoughts. Work out ways of responding to these triggers ahead of time. For example, if someone tends to take credit for your ideas, prepare to say with a smile, "I'm glad you like my idea."

Resentment Part 4: Ten Ways to eliminate resentment.
"I do it all and I get no recognition."

Research shows that putting intentions in writing helps a person achieve his or her goals. So the most effective way to improve your responses to hot button moments is to personalize the following ideas that are most relevant to you and write down how you plan to respond in the future.

Speaking up

1. Speak up when you think you should. People who have personal power are willing to express their ideas and opinions. They also respect and listen to others.

2. Act responsibly and hold others accountable for their actions.

3. Don't take it personally or act embarrassed if anyone belittles you. Remember that people who belittle others often feel inadequate themselves. Say something about it at an appropriate time. Most people will feel better about themselves if they can't get away with rude behavior.

4. Think about what you need and ask for it — it's better than complaining or talking behind somebody's back.

5. Take courage by focusing on what you have to gain in a situation rather than on what you have to lose.

Helpfulness and Appreciation

6. Don't agree to do things for people who take advantage of you. Just say you don't have the time.

7. Seek collaboration rather than doing everything yourself. It's much better to ask, "Can you help me with this?" with an upbeat attitude than to feel bitter about doing all the work.

8. Focus on helping those who appreciate you, and stop trying to get the attention of those who reject or ignore you.

9. Ask for appreciation in a positive way. For instance, "Isn't this a great dinner I made?"

10. Limit or end a relationship if you are the only one who is making an effort.

If you plan ahead how to respond with personal authority, it will become easier to avoid situations that give rise to resentment. It will also enable you to forgive past resentments and to stop holding grudges.

The Harsh Inner Critic: "I'm such an idiot for telling her I love her on the first date."

An inner critic is necessary

We all have an inner critic, which is necessary to stop us from engaging in illegal and unethical behavior and saying and doing outrageous things. Many people have an inner critic that can be abrasive in a couple of select areas, interfering with their ability to enjoy life in those areas by insisting that they are not good enough, attractive enough, or smart enough.

A harsh inner critic is harmful

Some people have a *tyrannical* inner critic, which can be debilitating. Too much self-criticism can lead to overwhelming feelings of inadequacy and depression, preventing full participation in life. When a person's inner critic becomes abusive in any area of life, it needs to be toned down, put in perspective, and transformed into an encouraging supporter.

Developing a constructive inner critic

Whether your inner critic is overly zealous frequently or only on occasion, we can learn to enjoy life better when we transform a ruthless critic into a helpful ally. Self-criticism is only useful when we consider our mistakes and use them as lessons to help guide us in the future. It is not beneficial when we punish ourselves for making a mistake.

So every time you say, "I'm an idiot," "I totally blew it again," or any other self-demeaning phrase, follow it with a positive phrase or a helpful and constructive thought, such as the following:

- "No one's perfect."
- "Everyone who tries makes mistakes."
- "What can I learn and take away from this experience?"

- "At least I'm romantic, but next time I won't say I love you on the *first* date."

Infatuation or love?

Regarding a declaration of love on a first date, there is a happy medium in healthy relationships between being emotionally withdrawn and sharing every fleeting feeling. Next time, maybe just say that you're having a great time, or simply enjoy the feeling of infatuation for a couple more dates before calling it *love*. Keep in mind, there are a lot worse things than announcing you're in love on the first date.

Positive Projection: "He is so amazingly intelligent and articulate!"

When desirable qualities such as intelligence, creativity, or leadership ability are incompatible with one's self-image, they often get projected onto others. Positive projection is frequently an integral part of falling in love. Carl Jung maintains that all impassioned, almost-magical relationships between people involve projection. The other person becomes the object of great love or loathing, and sometimes both.

We usually don't recognize our own projections because they originate in the unconscious, and they get projected onto someone with a suitable hook. For example, a person found to be "amazingly intelligent and articulate" is probably quite intelligent and articulate.

Then how do we distinguish a projection from an objective observation? Objective observations lack the feelings of awe, adoration, and reverence that attend projection. When we are projecting, whether negatively or positively, a lot of heat and emotion accompany that projection. The difference can be seen between "He's very intelligent," and "Wow! He's *amazingly* intelligent!"

Projection is not terrible. It's part of life. But the sooner we become aware of our projections, the better we can avoid some of their negative consequences.

Here are some of the problems with projection:

1.   It limits objectivity. Projection often prevents people from objectively perceiving themselves and others. Overly romantic illusions can lead to crushing disappointment and feelings of betrayal because we haven't assessed people realistically.

2.   It limits personal development. Unconscious content that is projected onto another person becomes less accessible for personal integration. "She's the articulate one." "He's the great planner; so he decides where to vacation." "She handles the finances because she's terrific with money." The implication is that "I am not good at that." Often positive projection causes people to hold back from developing the admired qualities in themselves.

3.   It results in too much dependence. When you think that your partner is great at something that you are not good at, you tend to depend on him or her to undertake that task rather than to learn how to do it yourself. "He'll handle the finances; he's good at that." "She'll speak to the children; she's good at that." When you disown certain attributes in yourself, you become lost without the help of others. Too much dependence will handicap an otherwise capable person.

4.   It leads to deep disappointment. Sooner or later the person on whom you are projecting admirable qualities won't be able to live up to your expectations. This can lead to disappointment, frustration, and loathing.

Realism

You cannot avoid having projections. However, when your feelings toward someone are intense, you can step back and consider whether you are idealizing the object of newly found affection. If you recognize that reality will offer some sobering surprises, you can still enjoy the endorphin rush of being in captivated by someone new while keeping your expectations somewhat realistic. When you recognize that your idealizations are exaggerated, you will be less disappointed when the other person isn't quite so amazing.

Self-development

Having positive projections is healthy and normal. Yet we must make sure that our projections gives us something to aspire to rather than hinder us from our aspirations. When you pay attention to your projections you gain an opportunity to discover the traits you want to develop within yourself. Your projections can be of great value because they help you realize that the talents of others that inspire you have been dormant in *you* all along.

For instance, the awe with which you admire his "amazing intelligence and ability to speak well" might indicate that you value, but disown, those attributes in yourself. Viewing your projection in this way informs you that you have an inner desire to develop your intelligence and your eloquence.

You can take steps to develop these traits by taking classes, reading, and practicing public speaking. Before long and with consistent practice you will discover that you had those skills available to you all along. Making conscious your unconscious projections won't prevent you from admiring others. But it may allow you to purposely develop qualities in yourself that you had no idea you possessed.

Respect each other: "He is always talking down to me."

The most indispensable quality in a relationship is respect. When two people deeply respect each other as human beings, they can deal with a lot of challenges and differences of opinion.

The greatest threat to mutual respect is a person's fears and needs that often manifest themselves as controlling, demeaning, or passive-aggressive behavior. While it's fine to disagree or to be angry, there must be an underlying sense of respect for the relationship to thrive.

It is absolutely critical not to talk to one another with contempt. When one person starts speaking disdainfully, with a sneer or a sense of superiority, the other needs to make sure it doesn't continue. It's up to you to make it perfectly clear that you won't take it.

When someone belittles you or attacks you verbally, you must set a definite boundary. Say meaningfully,

- "Please, don't speak to me that way,"
- "This discussion is not working for me," or
- "Excuse me?"

Love based on respect requires a sense of self-respect on your part. People who demonstrate self-respect tend to get respect from others. Not only is respect the foundation of a good relationship, it can be a powerful aphrodisiac.

"Why do you need to go back to school?"

Feeling threatened

Feeling threatened by your partner's growth and education is usually based on a fear that your partner will grow beyond you. Rather than discouraging your partner, use that fear to push yourself to improve and grow yourself.

Encouraging your partner

There are great benefits to encouraging your partner's pursuit of passions, whether that means studying the ancient Greeks or learning how to paraglide. There is nothing more loving and irresistibly attractive than having someone support you and believe in your endeavors and interests.

Encouragement also promotes a desire to reciprocate. When your partner encourages you to pursue your interests, you'll want to encourage his or her pursuit of passions as well. Taking on challenges builds a healthy confidence and vitality that will enrich both your lives.

Would you rather be with someone who's waiting for you at home weary and apathetic or someone with enthusiasm for learning — someone like Buzz Aldrin, who once said, "I have two passions: space exploration and hip hop"?

"I'm tired of being treated as a sex object!"

People who are verbally or sexually abusive should not be absolved from responsibility for their behavior. The victim should not be blamed for someone else's harmful behavior.

Yet there are people who complain of constantly being approached with sexual overtones, and they don't enjoy it. They wish they could be treated with more respect. While inappropriate and unwarranted behavior is inexcusable, they might want to take a look at whether and in what way they may be inviting others to view them in this particular way. Those who want a little less sexual attention might consider how they can curb such unwelcome behavior.

Self-perception

Early upbringing, cultural, and local attitudes toward groups of women affect the way individual women view themselves. Women may unconsciously take in these attitudes, which color their self-perception. They unwittingly convey their self-perception through their demeanor, dress, and body language, sending cues as to how they expect to be treated.

Women who are more prone to being treated as sex objects often have an expectation that they will be treated that way. Some seek out that kind of attention, as it may be the only way they know to get attention or validation, and validation of any kind can feel good. Some may dress or carry themselves provocatively, while others may not. Yet their body language communicates more powerfully than the clothing they wear.

Women who are treated like *sex objects*, which differs from being seen as sexy, seem to have one thing in common. They don't view themselves as deserving of respect for being *more* than sexy, that is, for being valuable, *whole* individuals.

Responding to sexual innuendo

A woman who views herself as a worthwhile, whole human being, including being sexually attractive, is less likely to pull in a purely sexual response. Even if someone were to make a sexual comment, she would feel *neither excessively flattered nor defensive about it*. If an inappropriate comment were made, she would view it as a reflection of the person making the comment rather than a reflection of herself.

Breaking the cycle

1. Become aware of how you may unconsciously invite others to view you in that specific way.
2. Neutralize your reactivity to such behavior, which will neutralize others' overly sexual response to you.
3. Gravitate toward people and situations that don't objectify you specifically or women in general.
4. Develop and value other aspects of your personality — for example, your intelligence, your talents, your inner strength, or your search for greater meaning.

Aging: "I hate getting old."

I feel like an 18 year old. I just can't catch her.

~George Burns

My mother Ros recently turned 82 years old, and has consistently shown everyone around her how kindness, a passion for life, and a can-do attitude is a fulfilling way to bring vitality to her own life and to those around her.

Her ability to look for the positive and the possible is what keeps her happy, energetic, and a joy to be around. People who are engaged in life and the people around them generally age well despite the inevitable signs of age as they grow older.

When my mother's new hip kept her on crutches off and on for five years, she would still walk on the beach daily. Even on crutches, she would ask what she could do for others, rather than be demanding of them. The moment her hip finally healed, she was back to ballroom dancing and skiing.

A shoulder injury caused her to start playing ping-pong with her non-dominant hand. She viewed it as a challenge and she has become quite difficult to beat even when she plays with her left hand!

She challenges her mind in many ways doing things for others, participating in the world, and following her passions. For instance, she plays the piano and translates her books into German — the language of a country she hasn't lived in for over half a century. She gathers together new and old eclectic friends at her table for lively discussions and a delicious meal. You may find her on a ladder painting my sister's fence, or helping her condo association's gardeners with weeding and planting.

With such enthusiasm and industriousness, her life seems better than ever. Given her kind and intelligent face, her beauty radiates through decades of collected wisdom.

> *Success is peace of mind that is a direct result of self-satisfaction in knowing that you did your best to become the best you are capable of becoming.*
>
> ~Coach John Wooden

Valor: "The firefighters of 9/11 were real heroes. What can I ever do that compares to that?"

So what I really meant was...

"What an inspiration they were to have risked and sacrificed their lives for others!"

What can I do?

Every day, I have the opportunity to make decisions — big and small — to be the best person I can be.

We'll never know which decisions or actions might have a powerful impact on other people's lives. It may be a smile, a job well done, speaking up for someone, or choosing not to speak that improves the life of another person.

> *Courage is what it takes to stand up; courage is also what it takes to sit down and listen.*
>
> ~Winston Churchill

"Were you out on the golf course again? I've been here alone all afternoon!"

Balancing togetherness and autonomy

To sustain a long-term passionate relationship, we need to balance two primary drives — the desire for togetherness and the desire for autonomy. While everyone has a different ideal balance point, it's clear that the extremes of too much togetherness or too much independence can each generate their own problems.

The cost of controlling someone

You might be able to get your partner to stop pursuing his or her passion of choice, but first ask yourself the following questions:

- Do you want the person you love to stop doing what he or she is passionate about? If so, is that really love or is it possessiveness?
- Do you want to spend time with someone who feels guilty, constricted, and resentful?

The fastest way to suck the life out of a relationship is to make someone feel guilty for what he or she is passionate about.

Moreover, no one can ever possess rights over another person. By cleverly controlling your partner, you can manipulate him or her into doing what you want, but you won't be getting the best of that person or the relationship.

The benefits of empowering yourself

When you feel threatened by your partner spending time apart from you, ask yourself how you could empower yourself instead of controlling your partner.

I recommend three steps that involve a simple change of attitude:

1. Be happy your partner is enjoying him- or herself. You will have a better relationship if your partner is happy.

2. Do something you enjoy on your own, whether it's reading Keats, going for a hike with friends, or taking up salsa dancing.

3. Make some positive plans together that your partner will want to participate in. "Let's have a barbeque tonight with friends." "Do you want to go to the river and try this great bottle of red wine tonight?"

Nothing can be gained by resenting your partner's passions!

Road Rage: "That blankety-blank cut me off! I'll show him!!"

What does the way you drive say about you?

Are you a considerate driver who will let another driver cut in if she's in the wrong lane? Or are you an impatient driver who tails other cars, gets angry, and swears when people cut you off or drive too slowly?

Your driving could say something about your own *shadow*, that is, the part of you that has not been developed or is being repressed.

Always rushing

Two types of people typically feel aggressive behind the wheel. The first is someone who has trouble with simply being present, someone who is always impatient to get something done. This type feels a lot of pressure to get where he or she is going to accomplish goals and avoid "wasting time."

Lacking personal power

The second is someone who hasn't developed much personal power. When your self-empowerment lies in the shadow, it erupts in aggressive, inappropriate, or unattractive ways. When someone cuts you off, you take it personally.

When you're in a car and feel anonymous and powerful, you can become more aggressive without being concerned about what someone you know might think.

What can you do if you are one of these kinds of driver?

Practice relaxing into the moment

If you have trouble relaxing when you're not productive, work on simply relaxing into the moment. Breathe deeply, listen to music, or plan an event. Replace futile thoughts such as "Look at this horrible traffic; I'm so late!" with more productive or calming thoughts, such as, "There's nothing I can do about this now. I might as well relax/focus on the meeting I'm going to/mentally reorganize my life-goals/enjoy a good song. In a year, I won't even remember being late. So why waste time agonizing in this moment?"

Gain personal power in everyday situations

If you are the type who often feels powerless in life, find ways to develop self-empowerment in situations where you are not behind the wheel. Notice when you feel meek and compliant, or when you are repressing your opinions. Try to speak up and integrate personal power in a calm and moderate way in every situation. If you develop more personal authority in your daily interactions with people, maybe you won't feel the need to be aggressive when you get behind the wheel.

Re-Visioning Psychology: "With all my psychological baggage, I feel like damaged goods."

Pathways of the soul

In *Re-Visioning Psychology*, James Hillman describes his view of psychological symptoms and pathology as the soul's means of getting our attention to stop and re-imagine our lives. Interestingly, the original Greek term "psyche" means "soul." Thus, psychology can be viewed as the study of the soul.

Hillman suggests that true psychological healing only begins when we focus on what an individual's soul seeks, not simply what the ego wants. Thus, symptoms give us an opportunity for "soul making."

The psyche may upset or disturb us with symptoms such as depression, outbursts, sleeplessness, eating disorders, conflict or worse in order to get our attention. The symptoms indicate that our soul is seeking something not yet attained.

Medical myth

Hillman holds that we are under the spell of the medical myth when we believe that psychological symptoms are something to be removed or cured.

Instead, psychological symptoms can be transformed when they are "re-visioned" as multi-faceted, human pathways of the soul. Pathologies are the means by which the soul gets our attention when we are missing the soul's intended journey. We must therefore investigate the meaning behind the symptom.

Healing fiction

Rather than simply trying to get rid of a symptom, one should ask, "What does this symptom want to say? Why has it arrived at this time? What kind of life am I leading that it needs this disturbance? What does the soul want?" Hillman proposes that the soul heals by telling itself a better story — a *healing story* that can dissolve the belief system that keeps the soul locked in misery.

This is not to say that we don't want to change risky behavior or remove dangerous symptoms. However, the symptoms are more likely to truly transform when you take time to look at the meaning behind them. For instance, in the case of over-eating, one might ask, "Why am I never satisfied? What nourishment is my soul seeking that would satisfy it?" Seeking to be filled up by food may be a metaphor or substitute for the nourishment the soul is seeking.

Imaginative consciousness

Hillman's "Archetypal Psychology" requires a re-directing of psychology away from logical analysis into the inner empathic meanderings of the heart. He claims that soul-work is grounded in an aesthetic, poetic basis of the mind. The "crazy artist" and the "mad scientist" are metaphors for the intimate relation between pathology and imagination.

The soul speaks the language of imagination through images, music, and metaphor. Therefore, to discover what the soul wants we need to pay attention to our imaginative consciousness. Ultimately, this will make the difference between feeling "damaged" and learning to live "soulfully."

> *Archetypal psychology...claims that it is mainly through the wounds in human life that the Gods enter...because pathology is the most palpable manner of bearing witness to the powers beyond ego control and the insufficiency of the ego perspective.*
>
> ~James Hillman in "Archetypal Psychology"

3. PERSONALITY TRAITS

Logical vs. Emotional: "He tells me to stop being so emotional. I don't want to be cold and unfeeling like him!"

The steadfast, unemotional husband, who at first is drawn to his warm, emotional wife, soon grows frustrated with the rollercoaster ride of her emotions. Of course the genders here are not fixed as these personality traits can go either way.

Polarization

Intrigued by one another at first, opposites sometimes end up loathing the opposing qualities that attracted them in the beginning. When each tries to change the other, both become more deeply entrenched in their own original one-sided behavior. In this example, he becomes cold and withdrawn; she becomes desperate for connection. Neither attitude is a great aphrodisiac!

We've all seen relationships where the emotional partner oscillates between gushing love and fervent hatred. The "logical" partner often protects himself from the volatility of his "emotional" partner by detaching himself from her, exacerbating her need for emotional connection until it becomes devouring.

He thinks himself capable of analyzing relationship issues logically and correctly. Yet his lack of awareness regarding his own secret prejudices and sensitivities can make his use of apparently cool rationality seem pernicious. As his partner finds it difficult to argue against his seemingly superior logic, her arguments become riddled with outbursts of irritation.

Here is a case where intense reactivity can lead couples to polar opposites. The extreme position of each partner scares the other into a more defended posture. Angry and wounded, they both retreat to their respective corners.

Integrating the opposite

If the relationship is to grow, each partner needs to integrate some of the contrasting quality to become more whole. Both partners need to accept the other's qualities, as flawed as they are, and move toward the center themselves. If one person becomes more balanced, the other is likely to follow, because there will be less need to be on the defensive.

If the emotional person were to respond with calm objectivity, it would allow the rational person to show more feeling without fearing that he will be sucked into histrionic chaos. If the rational person were to get in touch with and express some of his own emotions — discomfort or fear, for example — the emotional person would gain compassion for him, and no longer seek to get a show of emotion from him.

The Observer: "I like my privacy. I can do without people."

The Observer personality type

People with an Observer personality — one of the Enneagram's nine personality types — tend to stand back and observe rather than engage others. They live in a more isolated, private world to avoid the emotional stress that comes from interacting with other people. Many Observer types have learned to detach themselves from emotional connections and feelings as a way to defend themselves from psychic intrusion, rejection, or neglect.

Emotional distance

Observers often find escape through intense involvement within their mental world. Preferring to observe from a distance, they can be physically present yet they feel a sense of detachment. Their cerebral skills and competence seem to provide them security by

1. keeping them at a distance from the unpredictability of emotional contact, and

2. developing their mental understanding of the world.

Creating emotional distance protects a person from some of the pain of negative emotions. Yet it also blocks a person's ability to deeply feel positive emotions. Thus, observers often have difficulty feeling love and joy because they have protected themselves from feeling yearning and sadness. To be able to experience one side you must be willing to experience the other.

Develop physical and emotional awareness

How can people who tend to replace feeling with observation and mental analysis learn to handle and enjoy feelings? First they can make an effort to become aware of their physical sensations and emotional feelings. They must start by truly paying attention to what they sense and feel without moving immediately to mental analysis.

They can practice such awareness through body-work, such as dance, massage or yoga, or through artwork, gestalt therapy, or meditation with an emphasis on inner attention rather than detachment. By delaying the impulse to replace feelings with mental analysis, Observers can learn to stay with their feelings while experiencing less anxiety.

Gradually open up and reach out

Observers should also learn to recognize when they feel the urge to withdraw from others. It may not be safe to open themselves up suddenly or dramatically, as there is usually good reason that Observers have developed this way of protecting themselves from negative emotions. Yet through progressively increasing how much they open up and reach out to others, they can enrich their lives and relationships with greater emotional connection.

Developing the ability to feel more deeply should not take away from one's passion for contemplation and analysis. The benefits and pleasures of acute observation, thinking and mental analysis should not be negated. Life simply becomes more fulfilling as our skills and personality develop more flexibility and wholeness.

Rushing: "I'm only five minutes late and got so much done."

Many people get a rush out of rushing and squeezing extra tasks into every minute of the day. I personally have found myself feeling proud of all the things I can get done in a short period of time.

However, when rushing becomes a habit rather than a skill left for the occasional emergency, your life can suffer in several ways.

Problems with rushing

1. You cannot enjoy the peace of any given moment because your mind is already focused on the next task.

2.   Even if you enjoy the challenge of speed and action, you exude tension.

3.   Others feel your tension and don't enjoy being with you. They might in fact feel as if they are an imposition on you.

4.   You tend to make more mistakes and forget things when you rush.

5.   You spend less quality time with others.

Consider your effect on others

When you are overly focused on a specific goal, you may forget the impact you have on others. For example, people often tailgate while driving because they don't allow enough time to get where they're going. They were too busy trying to squeeze in an extra task.

Worst of all, people become impatient and rude with those closest to them if they have too much on their mind.

Be more present

Take a step back and notice your tendency to fill every possible moment. Become aware of the anxiety that it causes and consciously slow down.

There's no need to swing to a life of meditation. Simply take a little more time to be "present" to yourself and those around you. When you become more present, it's easier to resist the urge to cram in one more undertaking. Calming your inner pusher will allow you to experience greater serenity and depth in your life.

Too much Guilt:
"He makes me feel guilty if I don't do what he wants."

If we are going to be kind, let it be out of simple generosity, not because we fear guilt or retribution.

~J.M. Coetzee, *Disgrace*

Excessive guilt

Exceptionally considerate people often feel guilty for disappointing others even when their own actions are reasonable and appropriate. In these cases, feelings of guilt are excessive. Much of the guilt they experience may have been a learned response.

Excessive and inappropriate feelings of guilt cause people to experience unnecessary stress. They ignore their own needs, and surrender their personal power. In addition, people who are overly concerned about disappointing others become prey to manipulative people.

Feelings of guilt are like having symptoms of a cold. If you didn't know what the sneezing and headaches meant, you'd probably think you had something very serious. Once you know that you simply have a cold, the symptoms become more annoying than frightening.

It's similar when you experience guilt — you think you're doing something horribly wrong when you disappoint another person. However, when you realize that you were simply raised to consider other people's feelings as more important than your own, you can then learn to set aside excessive feelings of guilt.

Guilt trips

How do you respond to someone's unfair expectations of you?

Say, for example, an acquaintance wants to stay at your home for a few days, despite the inconvenience to you. He points out that he bought you coffee and that your apartment is conveniently located.

If it doesn't work for you to have that person as a guest, simply respond in a matter-of-fact way, "I see how you would like that, but that wouldn't work for me. Sorry." Or "I've got too much going on, but good luck finding a place." Smile if you want, set your guilt aside, and don't worry about disappointing people who use guilt to manipulate others. They will survive and you will feel better about yourself. The anxiety will pass.

Be clear

Don't expect others to know what you want. Some people are more self-centered while others are more considerate. In either case, you should not count on someone else to take care of your needs and desires. You have to take care of them yourself by direct, immediate, and matter-of-fact communication. Do not equivocate. You do not want to play guessing games with a few guilt trips thrown in.

The Persona and the Shadow: "I've always been accommodating, but at times I'm shocked at how mean I can be."

The Persona

Carl Jung gave the name *persona* to the part of the personality that identifies the role an individual chooses to play in life. An individual's *persona* is the impression he or she wishes or tends to make on the outside world. For instance, one person's *persona* might be the "responsible caretaker," while another's is the "fun-loving comedian" or the "suffering victim" or the "amazing jock."

We develop a *persona* early in life as a result of inborn personal attributes and interactions with our environment and culture. A *persona* is a necessary part of the personality that interfaces between our ego and other people. It also acts to protect parts of our inner self from the world. For instance, being tough or being funny are two different *personas* people develop to protect their vulnerability from others.

The *persona*, however, is only one part of the personality — the most visible part. Problems arise when an individual becomes too heavily identified with his or her *persona*. When a person identifies with only one aspect of the personality, other qualities become repressed and remain undeveloped. For instance, the fun-loving comedian might disown any sense of depth and seriousness. The strong leader might disown any sense of fear and vulnerability.

The Shadow

That which gets repressed or ignored in order to put forth the *persona* becomes an individual's *shadow*. The more we identify with our *persona* — that is, the more we believe that we *are* our *persona*, the more split-off the *shadow* will become.

A disowned *shadow* is likely to act out in destructive ways without our being aware of it — as when a person unexpectedly becomes mean or violent, acts out sexually, or falls apart emotionally. If you've ever said, "I don't know what got into me," or asked somebody else, "Where did that come from?" then you have experienced or witnessed an eruption of the *shadow*.

Example: the Accommodating Persona

When you identify yourself as being accommodating and believe that that's who you are rather than just a way you choose to behave sometimes, you disown the parts of yourself that are at odds with being accommodating. You may completely ignore any desires or opinions that appear "selfish" to you.

Repressing any feelings and behavior that may appear selfish to you increases pressure on the *shadow* until those feelings erupt suddenly, surprising you and those around you. The *shadow* may manifest itself in many different ways, as for example, nightmares, passive-aggressive behavior or sudden outbursts.

Similarly, someone who identifies with being powerful may find his or her vulnerabilities emerging as weakness, dependency, or panic, as we saw when Libya's dictator Gaddafi faced death and pleaded for his life.

Wholeness

Wholeness develops when we become aware of and respect all the dimensions of the self. We can then start developing unfamiliar parts of ourselves so that all those dimensions belong and can manifest themselves appropriately.

In order to stop saying mean things, it helps to become aware of your *shadow* — the part of you that is not always accommodating in this case. By acknowledging and starting to develop your unaccommodating parts, such as your own self-interest, power, and independence, none of which are bad in healthy doses, you can start the process of reconciling the diverse states of your personality. When you respect the parts of yourself that do not fit into your *persona*, they are less likely to explode as anger and irascibility.

All the different parts have a constructive role to play in your life. You can still choose to be accommodating, but it will be an authentic choice rather than an automatic response. Moreover, once you bring some light onto your *shadow*, it will be less likely to cause you pain and trouble.

> *The ego keeps its integrity only if it does not identify with one of the opposites, and if it understands how to hold the balance between them. This is possible only if it remains conscious of both at once.*
>
> ~Carl Jung, *The Nature of the Psyche*

Over-functioning and under-functioning: "If I don't take care of things, nothing will ever get done."

Emotional system

Every family is an emotional system where the functioning, behavior and beliefs of each person influence those of the others.[1] Over-functioning is different from simply doing kind things for another person or having distinct but equal roles and duties. It is an ongoing pattern of feeling responsible for the emotional wellbeing of another and trying to compensate for the perceived or real deficits in that person. It creates a re-enforcing cycle of dependence.

Polarization

The over-functioning of one person leads the under-functioning person to become dependent by entrusting responsibility for decisions and effort on those willing to do the work. As a result, the under-functioning person becomes less capable — creating a self-fulfilling prophecy.

As family members anxiously focus on compensating for the under-functioning member and trying to "correct" the problem, relationships become polarized. Examples of these polarities include "over-adequate" and "inadequate," "hard-working" and "lazy," "decisive" and "indecisive," "goal-oriented" and "procrastinating."

Resentment

The under-functioning person may unconsciously like the attention and being taken care of, and thus allows others to over-function. Yet often his or her increasing dependence and helplessness will lead to self-loathing. Meanwhile, the caretaker feels overwhelmed — "I have to take care of everything or things will go wrong." Resentment on both sides builds up.

Solution

The way out of such polarities is to work on yourself rather than to attempt to change others. A positive change in one person will have a positive impact on others, even though there may be resistance at first.

1.   Do Less

Those who over-function need to do less. When mistakes are made, the over-functioning family member must resist jumping in to take charge, fix things, and make motivational speeches. He or she must be able to handle the frustration of seeing others fumble around and do things far from perfectly. If they keep trying, failure ultimately leads to success.

2.   Gradual Change

Gradual change is often less shocking and deleterious than sudden change. If the over-functioning partner has been in charge of all budgets, financial decisions, and bill paying, it's wise to ease into sharing those duties. Remember that both of you participated in creating the problem and it will take time to resolve.

3.   Explaining Change

Over-functioners may want to explain to the under-functioning family members that they realize that their own well-intentioned over-functioning has contributed to the current unsatisfactory situation. Then they must stand back a bit and allow others to become more autonomous, make mistakes, suffer consequences, develop resilience, and choose their own individual paths.

Example: Teenager Laundry

If the over-functioning parent has been doing all cleaning, cooking, and laundry for the teenagers in the house, it's helpful to explain how and why you'd like them to start doing their own. Teenagers like the idea of independence, although they resist doing boring chores that are the essence of being independent.

Explain that such changes are intended to help them become more capable and independent as they will be moving out in a few years and need to develop the habit of taking care of themselves. "Embrace chores, as they are at the core of becoming independent!"

Then you can either let their dirty laundry pile up in their closets, or tell them you won't drive them, or they cannot have some other privilege until they've done their laundry or other chores. In either case, the consequences of not doing their own laundry will eventually provide its own motivation.

Balance and Harmony

After initial resistance, those who under-function will gain more autonomy, especially if those who over-function allow them to suffer the natural consequences of their inaction. Although it's hard work to break patterns, eventually, with more emotional separation and autonomy, a better balance of capabilities and contributions in the household will bring much needed harmony to the family.

Developing Defense Mechanisms (Part I): "My parent was controlling."

It is surprising how many of the "choices" we make are not made by choice at all, as we are frequently driven by unconscious forces. Our automatic responses have been programmed out of necessity when as children we were trying to get our needs met.

Depending on their personality, children who have a parent who is engulfing, controlling, or hovering tend to develop one of the following belief systems as a means of surviving or thriving in their family system:[2]

1. Compliance: "I should be sweet, self-sacrificing, and saintly."
2. Power complex: "I should be powerful, recognized, and a winner."
3. Avoidance: "I should be independent, aloof, and perfect."

Each of these responses can be appropriate in the right circumstances. However, problems arise when a person favors only one response in most circumstances.

1.   Compliance

Accommodation is an attempt to appease other people by anticipating and complying to their wishes. While compliance can be thoughtful and appropriate, it is not healthy when it becomes reflexive, automatic, or leads to danger. In extreme cases, compliant people feel they have no will of their own. They become totally dependent on what others think, expect, and want of them. This can lead them to allow harm to come to themselves and others.

2.   Power Complex

Assertive behavior is an attempt to get control. We need to be self-empowered, but when power becomes one-sided or unconscious, it becomes aggressive and harmful. In the extreme you get the sociopath who must be in total control and disregards the welfare of others. Dictators, autocrats, and abusive spouses exhibit the power complex in the extreme.

3.   Avoidance

The withdrawing person steps away from anything threatening, and suppresses reflection about difficult issues. At times, this can be a smart move, but not when it is done in every situation and without conscious choice. People who respond with avoidance often unconsciously perceive that other people are powerful while they themselves are not. In extreme cases, a person may become disconnected from reality or dissociative.

Self-awareness

Why do we bother figuring out what anxiety-management systems we use?

The moment we become aware of our automatic psychological reflexes, we open up the opportunity to change our behavior and make genuine choices. We can ask ourselves where are we stuck? What are these automatic defense mechanisms causing us to do that we don't really want to do? What are they preventing us from doing that we would like to do?

With an awareness of our unconscious belief systems, we can stop having knee-jerk reactions in certain situations. Instead, we can thoughtfully choose whether to comply, withdraw, or assert ourselves, among other possible responses. When we start responding differently, we can transform our old patterns to new kinds of behavior and consciously choose our course of action.

Developing Defense Mechanisms (Part II): "My parents never cared about me."

Close familial relationships create an environment where it is quite normal to develop mild defense mechanisms. These defenses are healthy when used in a conscious and thoughtful way. However, when they cause us to react unconsciously or in an extreme way, they eventually will create problems in our relationships and limit our life choices.

Generally, people experience a parent as either too involved or not involved enough. In the first case, the parent may seem controlling, overwhelming, or hovering. In the second case, a parent may seem indifferent, under-involved, or absent.

Abandonment

A child develops certain defense mechanisms in response to an under-involved parent. Extreme under-involvement is experienced by the child as abandonment. This includes not only parental rejection and indifference, but also environmental insufficiency — for instance, poverty, prejudice, or a wartime childhood.

Children tend to engage in magical thinking, which causes them to conclude that the world around them is a message about them. "If my mother neglects me, I must be bad." "If I am poor and never have enough food, I must be unworthy." This kind of thinking based on a sense of lack leads to four typical responses, the first two of which involve internalizing poor self-esteem.[3]

Four typical defense mechanisms

1. Self-sabotage

Self-sabotaging behavior is when "you are your own worst enemy" and find yourself taking actions to ensure that you will not succeed. You have internalized the message that you ascribe to your parents making about you: *You are insignificant.* Patterns of self-sabotage develop as a way to confirm your resulting poor self-esteem — that *I am not worthy of success, happiness or good fortune.* The child feels a certain comfort in the familiarity of continuing to fail. For example, the child doesn't show up to take a test or fails to follow through on promises made.

2. Grandiosity

Grandiosity is an over-compensation for an unconscious sense of poor self-esteem. True grandiosity refers to an overblown sense of superiority, which often accompanies the narcissist. Mild doses of grandiosity include trying to prove you are worthwhile by driving an expensive car, having a big house, achieving many milestones, and developing an impressive outer appearance. Focusing on proving your superiority leaves little time for other less showy pursuits that are more fulfilling on a personal level.

3. Serving the narcissist

Some children have a parent who is unable to relate to the child other than to use the child's accomplishments to feed his or her own narcissism. Children with narcissistic parents who are stage-door mothers or hockey-team fathers may find that the best way to defend against a chronic sense of emptiness is to serve the narcissistic parent. Yet even when the child makes the parent proud, there's a feeling of lack in the relationship — an emptiness that says, "I am never good enough." Even after growing up, the children of narcissistic parents experience the sense that they are living someone else's life.

4.   Neediness

A needy person yearns for reassurance or validation in order to feel worthwhile. A longing to satiate insatiable yearnings can lead to serial relationships, excessive materialism, and other distractions. Such unquenchable longing can also result in addictions, which are often attempts to manage anxiety that comes from a feeling of emptiness. Despite these attempts to satisfy such craving, it never stops because the human spirit is not satisfied by addictions and distractions. Thus, the neediness continues.

Moving beyond our defense mechanisms

While our defense mechanisms originally served to help us survive or thrive in our childhood environment, as adults, these reflexive responses cause problems and limit our lives. Once we recognize that a defense mechanism may imprison us, we can learn to think twice before acting, and we can begin to make new choices to live the life we desire. Here are some suggestions as to how to start overcoming specific defense mechanisms:

1.   Overcoming Self sabotage

Often fear of failure drives a person to self sabotage. The key then is to go ahead and face less than perfect results. To resist the urge to stop trying and give up, focus on working hard rather than getting perfect results.

2. Overcoming Grandiosity

Engage some pursuits that don't involve self-image — such as helping others, individual sports, or reading for pleasure.

3. Overcoming Serving the narcissistic parent

To find out what it is that you enjoy, try pursuing friends and interests that have nothing to do with what your parents want for you.

4. Overcoming Neediness

Become aware of your impulse for instant gratification, whether that's through getting someone's attention or unnecessary consumption. Wait ten minutes before doing anything and the impulse may pass. Distract yourself with a more productive endeavor.

Only through practicing new ways of responding to the world can we develop true choice as to how we live our lives.

Narcissism Part 1: Symptoms of Narcissism. "My husband is so selfish! Is he a narcissist?"

Narcissistic Personality Disorder is characterized by extreme selfishness, a lack of empathy, and a craving for admiration. Freud aptly named the disorder after the mythological figure of Narcissus, who fell in love with his own reflection in a pool of water and was doomed to never receive love in return from his reflection.

Craving for admiration

There are degrees of narcissism, ranging from excessive self-importance to full-fledged Narcissistic Personality Disorder. It is natural to enjoy praise and admiration, particularly given our current media culture, which values recognition for image, power, and status more highly than wisdom, responsibility, or a sense of meaning. However, narcissists don't simply *enjoy* occasional admiration, they *crave* it. It is *the primary drive* in their lives.

To obtain the praise and admiration they seek, they will exaggerate their talents and accomplishments. Their desire to be viewed as superior can lead them to misrepresent their history and their accomplishments. They may lie and cheat in order to get promotions, win competitions, or seduce people.

Self-aggrandizement

Narcissists are preoccupied with self-aggrandizement. They work very hard to hone public opinion of their image. They seek power, fame, status, or money, and are often envious of others who have an abundance of these resources. With arrogance that reaches grandiosity, they demand that others treat them as special and superior.

Socially-manipulative

High-functioning narcissists present themselves well and are socially adept, working hard at creating a praiseworthy image. In casual relationships, they are likable. However, in intimate relationships, they frequently display envy, arrogance, and entitlement. They protect themselves from criticism, humiliation, and rejection by over-reacting with contempt or outrage. Underlying all these emotions is often a feeling of emptiness.

Behaving with entitlement and lacking in empathy, narcissists tend to exploit others to serve their own desires. Focused on their own needs and frustrations, they become skillful at controlling and blaming others. As you can imagine, superiority and entitlement do not promote mutually-satisfying, long-term close relationships.

Avoid becoming dependent on a narcissist

You cannot change narcissists as they rarely, if ever, believe they need to change. Someone close to you may be truly narcissistic or merely selfish. In either case, you will need to take care of yourself to avoid getting hurt, taken advantage of, and exploited.

You can't expect a narcissist to set the boundaries you need to protect yourself. Nor can you expect narcissists to fulfill your needs and desires, unless it suits their goals. Generally you should not count on anyone to fulfill your deepest needs and take care of you, and this is particularly true if you're dealing with a narcissist.

You can enjoy a narcissist's charisma and accomplishments best if you avoid putting your trust in him or her, keep your expectations low, and remain financially and emotionally independent.

Narcissism Part II: Causes of Narcissism. "I don't have a problem with self-esteem!"

Narcissism is basically a psychological coping mechanism for people with low self-esteem. This may be hard to believe because the narcissist believes that he or she has high self-esteem. Moreover, his or her public persona seems to convey self-confidence.

Healthy phase of narcissism

Young children need to experience healthy narcissism to feel good about themselves, to gain the confidence needed to grow up and take care of themselves, and to be able to initiate social interactions. During the healthy phase of narcissism, children naturally feel they are the center of the world.

Children generally grow out of this narcissistic phase if they experience both *mirroring* and *idealization*. *Mirroring* means receiving empathy and approval from a parent or caretaker. *Idealization* entails looking up to a caregiver as a respected person separate from oneself.

Sometimes children do not grow out of the narcissistic phase because there was either no mirroring or no idealization.

No Mirroring

Lack of mirroring occurs in one of the following ways:

1. Approval is erratic or lacking all together. The child is ignored or abused.

2. Admiration is unrealistic, while realistic feedback is lacking. "You're the best, cutest, smartest...."

3. Criticism for bad behavior is excessive. "You are bad, evil, stupid!!"

4. Permissiveness and overindulgence are excessive, which ironically often result from a lack of caring. "Sure, have a bowl of candy, more juice, toys, throw your food if you want to, I don't care." They grow up in an environment without boundaries.

No Idealization

Children are deprived of idealization when they grow up in one of the following environments, all of which leave the child lacking in someone to look up to and emulate:

1. The parents are unpredictable, unreliable, or lacking in empathy.

2. The parents are emotionally or physically abusive.

3. The parents have no interest in the child's needs, but exploit the child to feed their own self-esteem.

Without receiving empathy or developing the ability to look up to others, children do not develop empathy for themselves or others. Consequently, they may grow up being psychologically stuck in the narcissistic phase, where primary focus in their lives is seeking admiration from others.

Deep-seated feelings of worthlessness

When children lack mirroring or idealization, they feel flawed and unacceptable. They fear rejection and isolation because of their perceived worthlessness. To avoid the resulting pain, they focus on controlling how others view them by embellishing their accomplishments and skills.

They feel deep shame, which causes them to develop an artificial self, their real self being unacceptable. While we all develop an artificial self to some degree, narcissists *identify* with their artificial self. Preoccupied with presenting the right image, ironically, they are rarely aware of their own low self-esteem.

Flaws are unacceptable

People with adequate self-esteem are usually willing to look at themselves with honest self-reflection and consider areas in which they could improve. This makes sense because they have empathy for the flaws and inadequacies in both themselves and others.

Sadly, the narcissist believes that flaws are to be loathed and concealed, and that only perfection and superiority can be displayed. Thus, they view themselves and others with a perspective that swings from over-valuation to contempt. In their quest for approval and acceptance, they use their charm and charisma. Once they are dependent on others' approval, the smallest hint of disapproval can send them into a state of despair or fury.

Avoid becoming emotionally dependent on a narcissist

To protect yourself from the emotional pendulum of the narcissist, it's best not to make your self-worth dependent on a narcissist's validation by perpetually trying to please him or her.

While the narcissist's charismatic charm might feel irresistible at first, it could soon turn into scorn and retaliation.

Narcissism Part III: Celebrity, Power, & Status.
"My spouse seems more narcissistic since his promotion."

Acquired Situational Narcissism

Narcissism brought on in adulthood by celebrity, power, or prestige has been called *Acquired Situational Narcissism*[4]. The attention received as a result of celebrity or prestige intensifies any *existing* tendency toward narcissism.

Adult narcissists with status or celebrity become more self-centered because of the favorable treatment and praise they receive. They thrive on attention and conclude from the fact that people fawn over them that their own satisfaction is what's best for everyone.

Praise and admiration boost the narcissist's self-esteem, but only temporarily, because it merely reflects the false self. The ongoing need for validation and adulation can never be satisfied. When faced with criticism or solitude, the shadow feelings of worthlessness grow in corresponding proportion to the need for admiration. To fight off this inner doom, narcissists double their efforts in pursuit of self-glorification.

Enjoying status vs. entitlement

Most people enjoy being admired or gaining status. Yet most people also enjoy relationships, learning, and pursuing passions all for their own sake, rather than as means to achieve acclaim. True narcissists, on the other hand, feel *entitled* to attention, and shamelessly pursue their desire for it *at all costs*. In extreme cases, they will exploit those in subservient positions and those assumed to be subordinate. Maids, interns, and employees are convenient targets as they are less likely to resist those with power and prestige.

Public vs. private

In their drive for stardom, narcissists hone the ability to exhibit socially appropriate behavior if it serves them to do so. In public, they may act like the perfect husband or wife, charismatically expressing admirable family traits such as warmth and devotion. In private, however, they may show little regard for the family's feelings or wellbeing. In fact, they can be sarcastic, sadistic, arrogant, and insulting.

Deception and lack of concern may cause the family to feel rejected, humiliated, and angry. It's important to realize that the negativity is not a reflection of the family members, but of the narcissist's limited ability to empathize with other people. The betrayals and attacks are not personal, but result from the narcissist's craving to be seen as superior even at the cost of degrading those closest to him or her.

Take care of yourself

It is vital for relatives of narcissists to protect themselves from denigration and contempt. A good first step usually involves pointing out how the culprit's actions are affecting them negatively. However, it's probably impossible to persuade full-fledged narcissists to change given their primary motivation to prove their superiority. It's better to know whom you are dealing with and then decide how to enjoy and/or limit your involvement in the relationship. It may ultimately be best to terminate it.

Narcissism Part IV: How to Deal with a Narcissist. "What about me?"

1.   Don't Trust a Narcissist.

Don't look for or expect intimacy with a narcissist. If you decide to enjoy the narcissist's charm and charisma, make sure that doesn't translate into trusting him or her with your inner secrets. Don't set yourself up for betrayal and hurt by having confidence in his or her loyalty. Don't let your feelings of self-worth depend on a narcissist's love, actions, or behavior.

2.   Speak to the Narcissist's Self-interest.

It is usually helpful to express your feelings or needs. However, if you're dealing with a true narcissist, don't expect empathy and understanding. It's more effective to show how something will benefit the narcissist's self-interest.

3.   Don't Disagree.

Beware of disagreeing with or contradicting narcissists. They behave as though they are confident and strong but they are easily offended. Their armor is shiny but crumples easily. They don't want to be found to be inadequate. Thus, if you confront their weaknesses, they may become vengeful and punitive. Keep your discussion focused on practical goals rather than personal accountability.

Here we see one of the reasons it is difficult or impossible to have a truly intimate relationship with a verified narcissist. Intimacy requires that we can be candid with one another disclosing who we are and what we think and feel, even if the other person disagrees. A narcissist's sense of self ironically is not strong enough to allow acceptance or disclosure of any of his or her vulnerabilities.

4. Be on your Guard.

Narcissists hide their own flaws and project problems, flaws, and mistakes on to other people. Beware of allowing them to blame you for too much. If you are doing business with a narcissist, keep a paper trail. In marriage or divorce, hire a good attorney.

5. Separating from Narcissistic Parents.

Narcissistic parents view their children as extensions of their own false self-image that they are busy presenting to the world. If the child disagrees or doesn't abide by the family image, narcissistic parents lose interest in or become hostile toward their own child. It's helpful not to take this personally, but to see that the parents' preoccupation with their own image and their callousness toward the child are caused by their low self-esteem.

6. Don't hope for Change.

It takes a lot of motivation for anyone to change. Unfortunately, narcissists rarely have the desire to change because they don't think they need to change. They also fear showing any vulnerability involved in self-reflection and transformation. They seldom seek counseling, but if they do go, they tend to manipulate the situation in order to look good rather than self-reflect to improve their lives.

When you realize how they are motivated, you can more easily choose whether to encourage the narcissist's self-image or not deal with him or her at all.

7. Avoid being Narcissistic.

We all have some narcissistic tendencies, and should therefore beware of becoming dependent on others for their compliments and approval to boost our feelings of self-worth. Psychological dependence on others comes at a cost. Reflecting about our own self-interest can prevent us from becoming overly self-centered.

There is a big difference, however, between being insecure or self-centered and having the condition of Narcissistic Personality Disorder. If you are self-reflective enough to wonder whether you are a narcissist, it's highly likely that you are not.

Order vs. Spontaneity: "Why do you have to plan all the time? Be spontaneous!"

The Greek gods of mythology are illuminating archetypes that reveal universal patterns of human behavior. Apollo (the god of sun) represents order, light, music, and rationality, while Dionysius (the god of wine) represents revelry and the release of inhibitions. Our Western culture is founded on Apollonian values of order. As the West is clearly in an Apollonian sphere, the Dionysian impulse fades to the background, losing favor but still there ready to erupt in excessive release.

Conscious awareness of both the benefits and risks inherent in the extremes of Apollonian order and Dionysian freedom allows us to navigate our lives through the pitfalls of excess. Each archetype has value, but taken in the extreme, can cause harm.

Different types of Order

Order and freedom are two of many deep-seated needs that often conflict with one another. Thus, people tend to favor one to the exclusion of the other. Some people manifest a need for order in their physical surroundings, requiring that everything in the home and the office be clean, neat, and organized. Some may adhere strictly to a financial budget and require that every dollar be accounted for. Some experience the need for order in terms of schedules and careful planning. Others are concerned that the roles in their various relationships are well defined. Finally, order may be experienced as a need to understand the world in clear mental constructs. For instance, rather than simply going out and skiing, the order seeker may be driven to understand everything about the technology of the equipment and the sport first.

Benefits of Order

Having order in one's world benefits a person by making life predictable, safe, and comfortable. Order also appeases anxiety about possible chaos and turmoil. Good planning and organization allow for more efficiency and productivity as well.

Problems from Excessive Order

Excessive emphasis on order drives out freedom, spontaneity, vitality and creativity. Too much order can lead to rigidity and lifelessness.

Freedom Lover

Those who favor freedom value creativity and spontaneity, while they reject being encumbered by rigid structures including schedules, budgets, housecleaning, or conventional rules. They may prefer intuitive thinking over academic study. They prefer to be moved by inspiration rather than by time constraints and rules. Some may not mind having a friend over if the house is messy. Some might not think much about the condition of their finances when buying things for themselves or others because it delights. They view the imposition of schedules, budgets, and order as rigid, lifeless, and boring.

Problem with Excessive Freedom

While freedom from structure can be exciting and unpredictable, excessive freedom leads to chaos and frustration. When others can no longer count on you, their disappointment saps some of that sought-for harmony in a relationship and joy of life. Too much freedom with spending can lead to financial ruin;

too many missed appointments result in loss of work and friends. Excessive freedom can lead to chaos in one's life.

Relationships

When both partners favor spontaneity excessively, the relationship may start with great fervor and passion, but over time, it can disintegrate into stress, chaos and ultimately, disappointment. When both partners favor order excessively, the relationship may look good from the outside — nice house, good jobs, money in the bank — but it may become sterile and lifeless on the inside. When partners polarize, each strongly favoring opposite values, there is either great dissension or passive resignation to their differences.

Integrating both and finding balance

Ideally, each partner in a relationship makes the effort to grapple with the tension of the contrasting needs for order and freedom within their own personalities. It's always helpful to integrate opposite qualities in small doses rather than swinging to the opposite extreme and getting completely outside of your comfort zone.

For example, if you are accustomed to buying dinner for everyone and buying what you like on a whim, start by trying to restrain yourself now and then. Consider a budget.

Or if you are accustomed to having a completely clean and organized house that looks like a model home, there's no need to invite all the neighborhood kids and dogs in at once. Yet you might start withstanding the tension you feel when a book or sweater is out of place. Start small and work toward a happy balance.

A benefit of integrating both values is that it's easier to understand and communicate compassionately with your partner and those around you. For instance, when one person understands the depth of the need for order and the fear of chaos underlying the desire for a spotless house, she can approach her partner with understanding, while attempting to point out her need for a little looseness and relaxation.

Changing balance

The ideal balance of Apollonian and Dionysian energies is not a happy medium between the two, but rather a fluid flexibility that takes into account the situation. At work, for instance, being on time for appointments is generally preferable to a come-as-you-please attitude. On a date, however, sticking to an early bedtime when the full moon is out and a romantic breeze is blowing might be a bad idea. Life ebbs and flows, opportunities present themselves and are gone. The appropriate proportion of control and release, which depends on all the circumstances, should be in constant flux.

Four problems with helping too much: "I'm just trying to help!"

People who habitually put others first and go out of their way to help them often don't stop until they become exhausted or ill. This can be detrimental to the helper, and ironically, it can also be tiresome and enabling to the people being helped.

Being helpful to others is a wonderful trait when it's practiced in moderation, appropriately, and reciprocated at least occasionally. If your primary focus is on meeting other people's needs, here are four questions to ask yourself to determine whether your helpfulness is excessive:

1. Are you neglecting your own needs and feelings? An indication of self-neglect is that you feel worn out. This is not

only unhealthy for you, but it puts a burden on those around you who now have to monitor that you don't over-work. This can lead to your becoming a burden to them — the last thing that you intended.

2. Are you becoming resentful even though you enjoy helping others? If so, you may be bending over backwards for other people too much. Although you enjoy helping others, you sense that the lack of fair mutuality is lacking. Although others may appreciate or even take advantage of your help, they may prefer spending time with someone who doesn't give too much unsolicited advice and help.

3. Are others offended by your help and involvement? Some super-helpful personalities may be surprised to learn that their acts of helping or pampering loved ones may be taken as an insult to their capabilities or as an intrusion into their personal space and autonomy. The recipient of your help may resent the unintended implication that he or she is incompetent.

4. Are you disabling others by promoting their dependency on you? By doing too much for others, you prevent them from doing for themselves and becoming more capable. You must allow others to do certain things for themselves, even if they first fumble and fail, in order to learn to become competent.

Take care of yourself first

Excessively self-sacrificing people can become more whole and improve their lives by learning to acknowledge and respect their own needs first. Notice that people who are the most enjoyable to be around tend to balance being considerate of others with taking care of themselves. It's easy and comfortable to be around people that you don't have to worry about because they take care of themselves.

Take a moment to assess

When you feel compelled to offer someone a glass of water, consider whether *you* may actually be the one who is thirsty. Then take a moment to sense whether others are the types who would rather get water for themselves. If so, notice whether you can simply *be* without *being of service* to someone else.

Truly being of service *is* a beautiful way to bring light into people's lives, but particularly so when it is done while honoring yourself and observing whether others would appreciate your help.

Clutter in the home causes clutter in the mind: "I don't have time to deal with this mess. My life is too hectic."

Your environment affects your state of mind

Clutter in your environment creates clutter in the mind and vice versa. Clutter in your home, office, and car tends to correspond to the clutter in your mind, relationships, and life.

Living in an environment where it is difficult to find things and difficult to think leads to chaos and indecision. In such an atmosphere, the anxiety of being overwhelmed by stuff stifles your focus and potential.

Accumulation of clutter has its basis in fear

Some people fear never having enough. People who have experienced deprivation during their lifetimes, whether through war, poverty, or hard times, understandably find it difficult to throw things out, fearing they may need them in the future.

Others equate possession with security. They fear not having enough. Somehow acquiring and retaining things makes them feel more secure.

Many people simply dread the task of re-organizing and removing clothes, papers, and stuff. They dislike the emptiness they feel when doing something so tedious. Instead, they focus on more stimulating activities — like shopping for more stuff.

Clutter is oppressive

By avoiding the tedium of organizing and throwing out possessions, you basically become hostage to them. Your possessions ultimately possess you and create chaos in your life. Disorganized papers, for instance, can lead to unpaid bills, fights about money, wasted time, and family disorder. A cluttered, messy home is depressing and weighs a person down with the burden it creates.

Making room for possibility

A de-cluttered home provides an atmosphere of serenity and potentiality. Yet there's no need to swing to the extreme of immaculate orderliness that may create a feeling of sanitary lifelessness. It's a *reasonably* clutter-free environment that creates harmony around us, and makes room in our lives for a range of new possibilities.

Enantiodromia: "My partner is too direct and he thinks I'm too polite."

Enantiodromia (en-ANT-ee-a-DROH-mee-a) is reminiscent of the Chinese concept of *yin-yang*, which maintains that each quality contains the seed of its opposite, and that absolute extremes transform into their opposites.

Carl Jung used the term *enantiodromia* to describe the emergence of the unconscious opposite of a personality trait into our behavior. When our conscious life is dominated by an extreme, one-sided tendency, life can flip unpredictably into its opposite, often causing pain and turmoil.

Too Polite

Let's consider the opposite qualities of being polite and being direct. The purpose of good manners is to make other people feel comfortable. Yet excessive politeness can make people feel uncomfortable. It makes them wonder what the overly-polite person is *truly* thinking and feeling, e.g., "What does this person want?" Extremely good manners can create an atmosphere of anxiety — a feeling of having to walk on eggshells.

Worse, under great stress, the true feelings of an overly-polite person may violently erupt because he or she has been holding those feelings in check. When those repressed feelings unexpectedly explode through the layers of politeness, everyone feels very uncomfortable — the very opposite of what the polite person desires.

Polite people can benefit from learning to be more direct when the situation warrants directness. They would be more effective if they considered what degree of politeness is warranted in different situations given the people involved.

Too Direct

The purpose of being direct is to communicate clearly with honesty and candor. However, an overly-direct person cannot be trusted to be silent, sensitive, or diplomatic when necessary. Extreme bluntness can be quite offensive and painful. While communication may be clear, in many situations it may not be the most effective way to communicate.

Thus, overly-direct people can benefit from adding discretion and good manners to their arsenal. Some situations call for bluntness — "Watch out for that car!" or "I simply can't afford it." Yet the key is to have the ability to choose your response after figuring out what would be most effective in a particular situation.

Gain flexibility

Communication is most effective when we have some ability to be flexible depending on the situation and type of people we're dealing with. So if you were brought up to be extremely polite and to never say a negative thing, learn to become more direct; people will respect you more. If you were brought up to "tell it like it is," you might benefit by being able to be more discreet and gracious around people who value courtesy and are worthy of your discretion.

"They say I'm too sensitive because I'm scared of my tough-guy uncle."

Growing up to become tough

Many people who seem to be tough and insensitive had childhoods where they had to hide the sensitive, empathetic side of their nature. If they showed any feelings of sadness, compassion, or fear, they got pummeled with criticism, cruel jokes, or physical abuse. Showing empathy or vulnerability became perilous. So they learned to repress such tendencies. They developed an inner critic that helped them to avoid showing any vulnerability.

This inner critic remains on high alert into adulthood, getting triggered by other people's vulnerability as well as their own. As a result of simply trying to survive in a tough family, they feel uncomfortable around those who show their sensitive side. You can see how someone who has had to protect himself from bullying behavior often becomes tough, and sometimes becomes a bully himself.

Empathy and vulnerability

Being conditioned to hide empathetic and sensitive impulses comes at a huge emotional cost. The ability to experience feelings such as sadness, fear, and helplessness is essential to developing compassion, empathy, and deep love for another human being. Someone who has repressed these feelings is bound to experience difficulty having empathy for others and finding love in their hearts.

A tough guy who scares others through verbal abuse causes hurt not only to the spirit and soul of others but also to himself. The fear felt by those around him has been felt by the tough guy thousands of times when growing up, which caused him to develop his protective shell. He had to live with it early on until he was able to numb himself to avoid the pain.

Embracing both strength and sensitivity

A healthy person develops *both* courage and heart. Take a look at many of the tough characters played by popular actors from John Wayne and Humphrey Bogart to Morgan Freeman and Harrison Ford. They're often tough and courageous, but they also feel secure enough to show kindness and compassion to others. They feel deeply and have the ability to get in touch with both their tough and soft sides and can draw from both. Regrettably, some people may never develop that happy balance.

Minimize your vulnerability around tough guys

Being sensitive can be a wonderful and humane quality. Yet in the presence of a tough guy, it's best to tone down your soft side so as to avoid triggering his abusive behavior. Emphasizing your touchy-feely side will only provoke him.

You can have empathy for a tough guy without becoming a target for his abuse. Tough guys feel most comfortable with people who can match their rugged persona. Ironically, only when they feel safe from being exposed as weak, do they sometimes let their guard down.

"I'm just not a sensual person."

Developing new parts of ourselves

We are all born and raised with certain attributes that we cultivate through practice, experience, and life-style. If you are born and raised to be a particular way, such as responsible, spiritual, or intellectual, but not sensual, it's not too late to develop your sensual side.

The purpose of life, says Carl Jung, is to *individuate*, which means to become more whole and multifaceted by developing all sides of our personality. Once we move into adulthood, we can choose to gradually develop the parts of ourselves we have neglected, whether that entails becoming more relaxed, more directed, more sensual, or more giving.

What is sensuality?

Sensuality means the enjoyment, expression, or pursuit of the physical, and being pleasing or fulfilling to the senses. Becoming more sensual does not simply refer to aspects of sex. Sensuality in relationship starts with the subtle interactions between people found in a glance, tone of voice, and body language.

People who don't feel sensual can develop their sensuality in some of the following ways:

1. Pay attention to all your senses. Take time to observe your surroundings, to fully enjoy every meal, and to smell the air. Observe others — their energy and mood.

2. Pay attention to your body, tone of voice, and facial expressions — how you feel and how you move and walk. Giving and receiving massages, and practicing yoga, dance, and sports are all ways that help you become aware of your body, your sense of touch, and movements. Learn to glide instead of stomp.

3. Practice being in the moment. Notice when you start thinking about something else rather than being present in the moment. Practices such as meditation can be very helpful in becoming aware of and transforming automatic thought patterns that prevent full presence.

Sensuality allows you to enjoy your surroundings and your relationships, as well as to notice subtle energy changes in yourself and others. When your perception becomes more sensitive, you can connect better with people and the environment around you. As a result, your enjoyment of the moment and all levels of interactions in your relationships with other people will flourish. When sensuality infuses your being, then fulfilling sexual intimacy is merely an extension of your enhanced awareness of the senses.

"I don't like many people in this town."

The extreme critic

The way you relate to the outside world often reflects the way you feel about yourself. If you tend to be critical of many types of people, chances are you have a severe inner critic that condemns many different parts of yourself.

The inner critic can prevent us from becoming a more multifaceted, life-embracing, and understanding individual. When we are overly critical, we disown parts of ourselves and constrict our life-force, which can in fact lead to depression.

An active antipathy for whole groups of people — as for example, tree-huggers, hipsters, nerds, jocks, the rich, or entire races of people — indicates a one-sided rigidity within your own personality that limits your empathy, your vitality, and ultimately, your life.

Develop empathy

There's no need to like everyone.

However, we can learn something from everyone. By comprehending *why* people are the way they are, our judgment becomes more nuanced, allowing us the flexibility and breathing room to live more expansively.

When you see or hear yourself starting to disparage whole groups of people, stop and ask yourself, "Does this feeling really benefit me? How could my life be enhanced if I let go of these negative judgments and stereotypes and pay some attention to the positive aspects of this particular group?"

[1] Kerr, M. & Bowen, M. *Family Evaluation: The role of the family as an emotional unit that governs individual behavior and development.*

[2] Reference and recommended reading: James Hollis.

[3] James Hollis.

[4] A term coined by Robert B. Millman. For an easy-to-remember acronym, try "Acquired Situational Super-narcissism."

4. RELATIONSHIP SKILLS

"Where have you been? You haven't called me in such a long time!"

So what I really meant was...

"It's great to see you. What have you been up to? Any good adventures?"

Always being right: "That's not what I said! What I said was...!"

When we find ourselves insisting on proving that we are right, it is time to look at what is motivating us. We often assume, sometimes unconsciously, that being right will lead to being respected, liked, appreciated, or admired. Generally speaking, however, the harder a person tries to prove he or she is right, the harder it is for that person to gain respect or appreciation.

The problems with proving you are right

Here are a few reasons for the disconnect between being right and gaining respect:

1. Adamant persistence to prove that you're right reveals underlying low self-esteem or feelings of inadequacy, which do not inspire respect or admiration.
2. In trying to be right, we disregard other people's ideas, causing them to feel ignored or hurt.

3.   Most importantly, being right generally comes with a condescending tone of voice that turns people off whether or not one is right. A superior tone of voice can trigger a defensive reaction in others, even when what's being said is completely logical and nonthreatening. If you've ever found yourself arguing over something ridiculous, you may find that you were reacting to a patronizing tone of voice rather than flawed logic.

Better than being right

One way to encourage others to consider your opinion is to use a friendly or neutral tone of voice. You'll feel more relaxed and others will feel more open-minded and amenable, which encourages a better response. You can even boldly disagree saying for instance, "This idea won't work," if you do so with a kind or neutral tone of voice.

If pretending is what it takes to change your attitude and use a respectful tone of voice, it's worth it. Remember that discussions that are *not* focused on one person being right are more stimulating and productive, and lead to healthier and happier relationships.

Setting Boundaries: "People walk all over me."

Have you ever longed for more peace, quiet, and solitude? Are you in a relationship with a person who is controlling, critical, or disrespectful? Do you get trapped in conversations with people who are intrusive or meddling?

Some people feel so uncomfortable creating boundaries that they end up enduring unwanted advances, abusive criticism, or long venting sessions. Others create unnecessary conflict by shouting "I need respect!" "Give me space!" or "Stop it!"

Boundaries are critical for sustaining respectful and fulfilling relationships. We all need boundaries and can create them in different ways. Some ways are more effective and less hostile than others. People who are best at creating boundaries often do so without others even realizing it. What is their secret?

They are people who know and respect themselves, and are sensitive and respectful toward others. They create boundaries through use of appropriate body language, energy modulation, tone of voice, and choice of words. They can often do so in a diplomatic way, though ultimately, they are willing to put their foot down to prevent unwanted behavior.

Creating Boundaries:

1.   **Open up gradually.** Don't give access to yourself when you first meet someone. Do so only very gradually. While you can be friendly and polite, be more thoughtful about opening up completely. Open up 20% instead of 80% until you have a good sense of who the other person really is.

     If you don't open up too quickly, there's no need to shut down your energy dramatically if things get uncomfortable. People are more likely to be offended if you are very warm and open, and then cool off suddenly. Take your time.

2.   **Recognize and respect your own comfort zone,** needs, and desires. Some people are so concerned with pleasing others, they don't check in with their

inner compass to find out what their own needs are — their need for

- respect,
- quiet,
- personal power,
- support,
- kindness,
- solitude,
- free choice, etc.

The sooner you are aware of your own comfort zone, the less likely you will let people go too far.

3. **Tune down your energy.** When you feel discomfort around someone intrusive, whether they are rude or overly friendly, cool down your energy. Be less open and receptive. You can subtly withdraw energy from the other person through posture, tone of voice, facial expression — particularly the eyes — and a palpable sense of withdrawal. For instance, look at the person less often and with less personal warmth.

4. **Cool down gently.** If someone is generally well-intentioned and you don't want to hurt his or her feelings, withdraw energy gently. That person will often sense it without consciously knowing what's going on.

    If someone does not sense your subtle withdrawal, cool your energy even more. If you still feel uncomfortable, you can verbalize your boundaries. For example, in a bar, "I'm sorry. I came here to spend time with a friend tonight." Then turn or move away.

5. **Refrain from being 100% open** about every feeling and thought even with your partner, close friends, and children. Keep parts of yourself to yourself. You

can be kind without being completely open (and therefore vulnerable). Take care of your precious vulnerability / inner child / inner life as if it were life itself, because it is.

While you don't want to lock away that part of yourself, be selective about when, with whom, and how much you share of it. Make it a conscious choice from moment to moment. You are never obligated to answer anybody's questions. When questions become intrusive, feel free to counter with another question, "Why do you ask?" Or, "I'd rather talk about something else right now."

6. **Express what you want in a positive way.** With friends and family, it's important to express your feelings. If you feel a need for boundaries, state your specific needs and make specific positive requests.

 Examples:
 - "I need to be alone right now."
 - "I need to calm down."
 - "I'm willing to talk to you if you would be polite."
 - "I'd like to figure this out myself. You may be right, but I'd like to make my own mistakes."
 - "I'd like it if you didn't speak to me with that tone of voice."
 - To your child: "I really enjoy spending time with you. I also need a little time alone to re-energize. So I'll spend an hour reading and then you can help me in the kitchen."

7. **Be less reactive.** Keep some feelings and ideas to yourself, OR, if you express them, do so from a place of calm. This is the opposite of being drawn into

argument and being reactive. Having boundaries means not being reactive or fused to the other person. It means not needing the other person's understanding and permission, but knowing what you want and calmly going after it. Often, the more you insist on boundaries in an angry or pleading manner, the clearer it is that you are not in control of yourself or your own boundaries.

Imagine a friend saying angrily, "Why don't you just do it the way I told you to!" An over-reactive response would be to say, "Stop telling me what to do! You have no idea what I'm going through." The better response would be to say calmly, "I appreciate your desire to help. But it's more helpful right now if you don't make suggestions," Or "Thanks, I'm handling this my own way. If and when I need help, I will ask you for it."

8. **Limit intrusive and draining conversations** and phone calls, particularly venting, gossip and complaints. A response to such unrewarding conversations might be,

- "Unfortunately, I have to get going. Talk to you soon."
- "Hi. I only have a minute." One minute later, "I have to go. Have a great afternoon."

For an ongoing problem that you'd like to address,

- "I feel a bit drained when we talk about these problems so much. I'd prefer to talk about something more uplifting."
- "I like to connect with you, but I don't have much time to talk with my commitments to work and the kids."

- "I'm sorry you're going through so much. I'd like to know what I can do for you. Do you want advice? Do you want me to point out how you might be participating in this ongoing pattern?"

- If the answer is "I don't need advice, I just need to vent," you can say, "Then I'm afraid I can't be of any help to you."

9. **Don't take without asking.** Taking food off someone's plate without asking is an example of fused behavior that is best avoided. Particularly at the beginning of a relationship, some people feel it's intimate and romantic to take food off each other's plate. The "what's mine is yours" mentality does lead to closeness, but not the type that's desirable. Emotional or physical fusion leads to control issues and resentment. Only when people remain emotionally and physically separate can they truly become more intimate. If you wish to achieve the best form of intimacy (whether between lovers, friends, parent and child) be sure to first ask, "May I try a bite?"

10. **Respect other people's bodies and your own.** No matter how many years you've been married, you are separate individuals, physically and emotionally. Acting as though the other person belongs to you conveys a lack of respect and lack of passion.

    Would you rather be treated as an honored guest or a thief in the night? Always seek permission when you touch someone. This doesn't necessarily mean asking permission with words, but look for the energy and body language that say, "yes." A little enticement may help as well.

11. **Respect a child's autonomy** regarding his or her body. This teaches children ownership of their bodies. Children who are brought up with parents who dress them beyond an appropriate age, impose unwanted affection, or don't respect their privacy, for example, do not learn to sense when their boundaries are being encroached upon.

12. **Be respectful and expect respect** both in public and at home. People who are critical or bicker in public are an embarrassment and irritating to be with. If a child, friend, or partner is inappropriately rude in private or public, it's important to express yourself calmly and firmly and be willing to leave if necessary. Public humiliation requires immediate attention.

If someone criticizes or mocks you, you might say calmly but seriously, "When you say that, I feel uncomfortable/sad/angry/like leaving. Please don't do that." If the person continues, it's important to be willing to calmly leave the situation, the restaurant, and perhaps even the relationship eventually. Once boundaries are firmly established, they are less likely to be encroached upon.

It's also important not to engage in an argument when there's no basis of respect. If someone attacks you, don't participate in the negative interaction. Try to respond without sounding condescending, "When you yell at me, it causes me to feel defensive. I'd be willing to discuss this if we can do so calmly and respectfully." Only with a prerequisite of respect can there be hope to achieve better understanding and improve a relationship.

"That's ridiculous! How can you believe that?"

So what I really meant was…

"That's an interesting point of view. Tell me more."

Or "Here's another way of looking at it."

When you put forth a genuine interest in understanding other people and welcoming their views, you set the stage to have a more lively, authentic discussion of ideas, rather than a tug of war causing offense and resentment.

On the other hand, if people in a relationship feel they have to agree on everything, their relationship will become stifled and lifeless.

An ability to discuss perspectives without hostility is key to having engaging and productive conversations. Such openness is of great value in problem solving, which is part of every day life, particularly if you want to lead a multifaceted and interesting life.

Pleaser and Receiver: "There's no pleasing him. The more I give, the more he takes."

Herman Hesse wrote in *Narcissus and Goldman* that in art and love, giving and taking become indistinguishable. Ideally, as Hesse suggests, both partners give and receive whole-heartedly for the right reasons without any strings attached.

One-sided giving or receiving

A common dynamic seen within couples is that one partner tends to please while the other tends to receive (the *Pleaser/Giver* and the *Receiver/Taker* dynamic.) These opposites attract each

107

other, because they are complementary. Usually, each partner in a relationship needs to develop some of the qualities of the other side.

Unfortunately, rather than developing the needed quality to become more balanced, often each partner becomes *more* one-sided and excessive as a giver or a taker. Such polarization results in the relationship becoming increasingly oppressive, the giver becoming exhausted and the taker unsatisfied.

The Pleaser

What's wonderful about the Pleaser is that he or she is considerate, thoughtful, and has the other person's wellbeing and happiness in mind. Such a person is compassionate and able to recognize and satisfy other people's needs and desires.

Excessive pleasing

Yet the Pleaser may excessively dote over the partner, which may cause the partner to feel stifled and overwhelmed by a burden of guilt. The Pleaser's underlying need to feel needed may cause his or her partner to withdraw. While it's normal to desire appreciation, when the Pleaser gives too much, whether it's out of selflessness or a need for gratitude, it becomes draining and uncomfortable for everyone involved. The Taker in this case comes to feel suffocated. Or the Taker may simply feel entitled, leaving the Giver to feel depleted. In either case, the Taker loses desire for the Giver because the Giver is doing too much caretaking, an antidote to desire.

Sometimes when people split up, you hear "How could he leave her? She did everything for him." As unfair as it may seem, that may be precisely the reason he left. When someone does too much for you, you can feel engulfed by the excessive attention and oppressed by a burden of guilt. You also have no room to feel desire for the other person.

What Pleasers need to learn

Pleasers need to learn to ask for and receive what they desire from others. They need to put value on their own health and wellbeing, and thus, to take care of themselves and to receive help from others. They also need to develop the ability to let others take care of themselves, and to make sure their giving has no sense of reciprocal obligation or neediness attached.

The Receiver

Receivers are able to fully enjoy receiving from others, which is wonderful for both partners. Receivers often feel self-contained and independent. They may not feel they have to do a lot to please others because they feel quite satisfied in themselves. In order to be someone who can receive in a healthy way, you have to feel worthwhile and good about yourself.

Excessive receiving

However, if someone simply takes and takes, without an ability or desire to give back, then there is a devouring quality in the receiving rather than joy and appreciation. A person who only receives and does not give to others has a sense of entitlement based on deficiency rather than self-worth. He or she is often selfish or greedy, and justifiably incurs resentment in those who continue to give.

Similar to the Grinch who stole Christmas, such people seem to fear that they will become empty or lose part of themselves if they give too much or anything at all. To stave off the psychological fear of insufficiency, they tend to hoard what is brought their way, and even then, it might never be enough.

What receivers need to learn

The solution for receivers, therefore, is that they learn to experience the pleasure and joy of thinking and doing for others.

They will become more whole and full by doing so. They will learn that sense of joy that accompanies helping and giving to others, and find that they feel more fulfilled than when they simply take advantage of others.

Living together Part I — Manners and Boundaries: "What's the matter with you? Look at the mess you made!"

Most of us like to come home to peace and harmony. If you want your home to be an oasis of tranquility, it's key that you have manners and boundaries. Here are some basic guidelines to living with other people:

1. Acknowledge others. Acknowledge them when they walk in the room. Say "hello" and "goodbye." Don't take people for granted. Say "please" and "thank you."

2. Stay calm rather than be reactive. If the person you're living with is grumpy, you don't have to fix the problem or take it personally. Give the person space if you can. If the negative energy is overwhelming, then leave the room or say something without being offensive. "You seem unhappy. Is there something I can do for you?"

3. Seek some solitude every day and give others their privacy as well. By clearly communicating your intentions and your needs — that you need to rest or catch up on reading, for example, — others will not take your isolation personally.

4. Look for the best in others and you'll probably find it. Look for the worst, and that's what you'll find. If you're the critical type, learn to let things roll off your

back. But if you're the type to avoid making waves, you probably need to speak up. The sooner you bring up behavior that upsets you, the more casual and easy the conversation will be.

5.   Communicate without judgment. All of us react quite differently to a friendly request than to negative criticism. Tone of voice and intention are more important than wording. "I feel a lot happier when the house is neat. I would really appreciate it if you'd clean up your dishes after you use them. And let me know if there's something you'd like me to do differently."

People in close quarters who are caring and thoughtful without being reactive or invasive can make living together a joy.

Living together Part II — Fairness: "Well, I'm not paying for everything!"

Be fair with others, but then keep after them until they're fair with you.

~Alan Alda

In addition to having manners and maintaining boundaries, being fair in what you contribute in a household makes a big difference in the enjoyment of long-term relationships. Here are a few guidelines that work for most people:

1.   Clean up after yourself. There's nothing so discouraging as living with someone who leaves a mess everywhere. Relaxed order, not sanitary perfection, is a happy medium that works for most people living together. People who are either sticklers

for perfection or extremely messy are often better off living alone or finding someone comparable to live with.

2. Be thoughtful, but beware of doing too much for others. While it's kind to cook or clean for others, doing too much without willing reciprocity from them may result in your becoming resentful.

3. Maintain your boundaries regarding personal property. It's nice to be generous with people who are respectful and appreciative. However, if someone "borrows" something of yours without asking, you might say, "I'd like you to ask me first." If people don't respect your belongings, they likely will not respect you. If they persist in "borrowing" without asking, take steps to secure your property.

4. Have clear understandings regarding finances, both your own and your collective finances. In temporary relationships, where society has no legal say, such as non-married partners, or renters who share a house, it is very important to have clear understandings that address bills, finances, and paperwork. Clearly define what belongs to whom and who is responsible for what. Even if you live with your best friend or the love of your life, you want to protect yourself and your relationship from the outset. A relationship is more solid and stress-free when there is clarity regarding finances.

5. Don't gossip. When you align yourself with just one person, if there are more than two in the household, others in the house may feel alienated. If you gossip about others, people will suspect that you gossip about them too when they're not around.

6.   Have a sense of humor. This is probably the most beneficial trait you can have in relationships. As William James put it: "Common sense and a sense of humor are the same thing, moving at different speeds. A sense of humor is just common sense, dancing."

Over-functioning: "I work so hard to give my family everything, but they don't appreciate me."

People who do too much for others often become frustrated with the meager reciprocity and appreciation they receive. The trouble is that when you over-function you often cause the polarities in a relationship to become magnified.

For instance, if one person handles all the planning of social events, meals, and travel, others lose interest in handling those activities. They also become less capable in planning because they have no experience. Moreover, they rarely fully appreciate the person who does all the work.

Another example is when one partner handles all the finances and the other partner gives up trying, the latter will become both uninformed and incapable.

Resentment

When one family member over-functions, the others become less capable and more dependent, both of which diminish their self-confidence. As a result, the people who do not participate in handling family life will end up only showing dissatisfaction, resentment, and annoyance.

The over-functioner is stumped and becomes bitter, because he or she has done so much! Soon, family members become more dependent and reactive to one another, which worsen their incapacities.

Remedy

The best way to remedy the situation is to stop over-functioning. You can be honest and say, "I've been doing too much and I feel overwhelmed and unappreciated. I now realize that I'm cheating both of us. You don't get to contribute your ideas and effort, and I feel as though you're not grateful enough."

Then ask for specific help *without expecting perfection.* Make sure you lighten up, loosen your control, and do not criticize — mistakes will be made.

It may take a while to transition — old habits die hard. The key is to back off doing too much, rather than to push others to do more. When there's a vacuum, it eventually will get filled.

Needy Dating: "Why didn't you call me? I've been waiting to see if we're getting together tonight."

If you have definite plans, call the person to verify the time. Or if you want to make plans, call, be cool, be positive.

But if you are simply hoping that a particular person likes you and will follow through with a vague promise, then keep wondering, but in the mean time, live your life. Don't wait by the phone. Don't check your text messages every minute. And definitely don't call to complain!

Keep your own life engaged. Vibrancy is always more attractive than desperation. You're only as interesting as the depths of your own passions and interests. Pursue your passions, work, and keep meeting people. Rent the movie *He's Just Not That Into You*. Enjoy your friends; enjoy your solitude.

Bragging on a First Date: "I graduated with honors, won the state championship in tennis, and drive a Ferrari."

Bragging backfires

People brag in order to impress others. However, reciting your résumé and accomplishments on a first date actually can do the opposite. It suggests that you are compensating for low self-esteem and feelings of inadequacy. It also attracts people who want you to pull them into a false sense of superiority.

Enjoy the conversation

1. Retain some mystery. It's actually more impressive and fun to meet someone who remains a mystery and who prefers engaging in conversation rather than in impressing others.

2. Relax. Instead of flashing your credentials and flexing your muscles, relax and be yourself. Be curious without interviewing aggressively. Balance talking and listening.

3. Be honest. If you disagree with an opinion, say so diplomatically.

4. Feel good about yourself. Flirting is healthy — although you don't need to go overboard.

5. Take it easy. Getting to know someone is like dancing together for the first time. If you jump into your

fanciest moves without getting a feel for your dance partner first, you will be dancing on your own.

"I want to be married by the time I'm 35. I'm going on a first date and want to make sure he knows I'm interested in a serious relationship."

Hold on. Instead of making your first date an interview to find the perfect mate, take your time, enjoy the moment, and see how you like each other first.

Putting all your hope in the future with any person, let alone someone you hardly know, is foolhardy and will scare others away. Excessive desire for marriage comes across as desperation.

While getting married might be one of your ultimate goals, be fair to yourself. It takes time to find out if someone is really for you. First see if you have chemistry together, enjoy spending time together, and share important values. The best way to discover such things is by spending time together, exchanging views, eventually meeting each other's friends and family, not by putting pressure to tie the knot with someone you hardly know.

On the other hand, continuing to date someone you don't deeply care for is shortsighted because it limits your options and wastes your time. There are better things to do than squander your time in a dead-end relationship.

"I am not good at confrontation because I don't want to hurt people."

Confrontation vs. being steadfast

Can you learn to stand up for yourself without being confrontational? Yes. You simply need to state your opinion in a respectful, matter of fact, and firm way.

It's admirable to want to treat people with respect and fairness. However, that does not mean giving in and giving them everything they want.

Imagine if you raised a child and your goal was to avoid confrontation. The child would learn very quickly that being confrontational is the most effective way to get what he or she wants from you. You would be training that child to become spoiled, demanding, and selfish. Fear of confrontation invites bullies to use confrontation to get what they want from you.

Giving people everything they want at your expense caters to their selfishness and will cause you to feel and become exploited.

Disappointment is inevitable

Disappointment may not feel good, but it is a necessary part of life. You cannot avoid disappointing others because you cannot control their expectations. On the other hand, you underestimate people's resiliency if you think they cannot handle a little disappointment.

The only way for a person to avoid disappointment is to never have hopes, dreams, and expectations. Yet these are what motivate our journey through life. Fortunately, people don't have to have all of their dreams and expectations satisfied in order to live a full and happy life. In fact, disappointment can be a positive force in that it may lead people to make needed adjustments in their lives and to truly appreciate the blessings they do enjoy. Thus, giving in to others to avoid disappointing them is an impossible and undesirable goal.

Improving Relationships: "This is who I am. Nothing's going to change."

Fixed mindset[1]

If you have a fight with your husband and think "This relationship is never going to work", then it probably won't. If your boredom and lack of desire cause you to wonder "Are we growing apart?" you're missing an opportunity to rekindle your passion. Moreover, you will probably repeat this pattern in your next relationship.

People with a *fixed mindset* about relationships tend to become either entrenched and combative, or simply give up when the going gets tough. Often they hide their feelings in order to maintain harmony, but this ultimately leads to resentment and disillusionment.

Change-is-possible mindset

When we view emotional intelligence as a set of skills that can be improved throughout life, we are much more likely to improve our relationships. Those who ask themselves "What do I need to learn to improve my relationships?" have relationships that tend to improve and deepen over time. The mere belief that relationship skills can be learned increases the likelihood that your relationships will improve.

How do we figure out what skills we could learn?

Pinpoint how and why a certain problem occurs. Then ask yourself the following questions:

118

1. "How am I participating in the situation?"

Considering how you participate in a given situation is different from blaming yourself for the problem. In order to improve a relationship, you need to understand how you may be contributing to a negative dynamic. You have little control over another person; you can only change your own attitude and reactions, which in turn may cause a change in the people around you.

2. "How am I triggering the other person?"

"Is it my tone of voice?" "Do I sound like I'm whining, complaining, or being controlling?" If you are honest with yourself, you can probably figure it out yourself. Otherwise, ask the person directly. If he or she can't articulate it, ask friends, family, or a therapist.

3. "How do I allow him/her to trigger me?"

Take a look at what tends to trigger you. When you become aware of your triggers, you have an opportunity to change your reactions.

For example, if someone's controlling tone of voice triggers the rebel in you, which makes the other person even angrier, you can choose not to rebel. Instead, you can choose to deal with it another way. It's amazing how an ingrained pattern simply vanishes if one party sincerely changes his or her reaction. Instead of sneering: "Don't you trust me!?" you might respond more neutrally: "You sound really worried, and I want to assure you that ...."

4. Focus on what works.

Instead of labeling the relationship *good* or *bad*, think about when the relationship works well.

119

Examples:

- "Our discussions are more productive when I bring up problems after she's eaten."
- "When I state the problem once, I get a better response than when I repeat myself and go on and on."
- "When I listen to her without interrupting, she listens to me."
- "When I tell him I love him, am not angry at him, but am simply overwhelmed by work, he doesn't get defensive."
- "When I tell him that he doesn't need to fix the problem, but that I feel better by telling him my problems at work, he seems relieved."

5.   **Look at problems as opportunities to learn new skills.**

Start by asking yourself the right questions.

Examples of questions to ask yourself:

- Does my spouse feel criticized? How can I express my desires and needs without sounding critical?
- Do we argue about how to spend money? How can we each discuss our fears and desires about money and security, and develop a mutual plan, taking into account each person's underlying fears and desires?
- Has the relationship run dry of desire? Maybe there is another underlying issue, such as feelings of disrespect, contempt, or being controlled. What can I do to develop and sustain an atmosphere of desire, appreciation and sensuality?
- Has the relationship become pedestrian and ordinary? What can I do to make the relationship feel special or even sacred? What actions and attitude would help?

- Do I find myself yelling or complaining a lot? How can I express my own desires and needs without sounding controlling or critical? This can be learned. (Dr. Marshall Rosenberg's book "Nonviolent Communication" is excellent for learning how to communicate effectively.)

- Is one person always late and the other always punctual? How can we deal with that problem structurally (by using two cars, for example), so the punctual person doesn't end up resenting the late person, and the late person doesn't feel pushed?

Conclusion

Those who think that a relationship can be improved through developing skills are more likely to have successful relationships. A *change-is-possible* mind-set leads to a desire to learn, to embrace challenges, to persist in the face of setbacks, and to see effort as the path to mastery. By learning from feedback rather than becoming defensive, we can aspire to engaging in increasingly fulfilling, loving and happy relationships.

"You're so irritable! Why don't you go TAKE A HIKE and cool off!"

Compassion

It often pays to give people who are irritable the benefit of the doubt. There may be a good reason for the way they are behaving.

You may want to ask the troubled person, "Did something happen at work?" or "You seem upset. Is there anything I can do for you?"

Sometimes just a bit of compassion is all that's needed to restore a person's equilibrium. Tone of voice and good intentions are key, as surly individuals can and will read criticism into anything.

Space

Give an irritable person some space. When they become rude, it's important to let them know that their attitude is affecting you. Setting your own boundaries is important when someone is short or brash. You are not doing yourself or them any good by allowing them to treat you badly. You are merely encouraging disrespectful behavior, which makes both of you feel worse.

Try not to become rude yourself. Give them some time alone and say something like, "When you're this irritable, it makes me feel miserable too. I'm going to give you some space. I hope you feel better soon." Or "If there is something you would like to talk about, please let me know."

Negative patterns tend to get worse unless a distinct effort is made to stop them. If this becomes an ongoing pattern, it is important to sit down and have a serious discussion.

"It's fine for us each to have some space. But I want to have a relationship where we spend some enjoyable time together on a regular basis and where we are civil to each other all the time. Is that something you want as well?"

Once you have candidly drawn a line, pay attention to see how the other person responds in words and actions.

Mild Depression and the Blues: "Stop being so depressed! You should be happy!"

A place for sadness and introspection

While optimism tends to attract happier states of mind, we should avoid being judgmental toward people when they are living through their darker moods. When a friend seems down, it's important to ask if he or she needs help or wants to talk about his or her problems. However, simply being there is often more beneficial than jumping in quickly to "fix" someone's state of sadness.

In addition to being compassionate, we need to be able to give others space to process their own emotional states. There is a place and purpose for melancholy, heartache, and disenchantment. In fact, the experience of sadness and loss can be a prerequisite for happiness.

Psychologist James Hillman claims that the *gravitas* accompanying mild depression may allow us to discover the depths of the soul. "It brings refuge, limitation, focus, gravity, weight, and humble powerlessness." Rather than giving in to a dark mood or blaming someone else, a person undergoing the blues has an opportunity to listen to what the unconscious is trying to say, thus making the unconscious conscious.

People who identify with being action-oriented sometimes completely ignore grief and loss. Those neglected feelings may gain energy in the form of a shadow that one day will erupt to the surface as emotional outbursts or deep depression. Mild and temporary depression can be a wake up call to the sleepwalker within us, allowing us to take time to mull over our life's journey.

Stepping in

When a friend's melancholy goes on too long or becomes severe, it may be time to show concern about his or her inability to get out of the depressed state. Dark moods push people away and prolong isolation and solitude, which can perpetuate a cycle that becomes increasingly difficult to break. If depression is leading to atrophy and degeneration, it's important to encourage the friend to get help and see a health care professional.

Being Pedantic: "You're too codependent. I'll tell you what you should do."

The Expert[2]

Have you ever delighted in sharing your expertise only to be surprised by a cold response? Despite your passion about a subject, you may unknowingly alienate others by a lack of connection or an attitude of superiority.

The mind is a wonderful thing. It gives us a sense of understanding and control in the world. Yet when we speak purely from the mind in its realm of logic, objectivity, and facts, we tend to lack personal warmth. Remaining in the realm of knowledge and facts can cause us to forget that both expert and novice are human beings with feelings and desires. When people feel as though they are information-receiving vessels to be filled, they may feel objectified, alienated, or simply bored.

Basing your identity on what you know

Some people who particularly value what they know have come to base their identity and sense of adequacy on that knowledge. Their sense of self-worth then depends on being in the position of an expert. When they are not conveying knowledge, they may feel adrift or inconsequential.

Even as a true expert, a professor for example, it helps to develop some warmth and ability to connect with people in order to effectively convey knowledge and sustain a mutually satisfying relationship. When two people can simply "be" together without teaching or being taught, the relationship becomes more energetically alive. This kind of energy causes people to feel more at ease whether they are in the position of expert or not.

The Psychology Expert

Amateur psychologists as well as therapists have to be particularly careful not to use their knowledge to preach to, decipher, or label others. Even when such labeling is accurate, it feels demeaning to be scrutinized, dissected, and analyzed. Being told we are dysfunctional or codependent doesn't inspire love, passion, or functionality. In fact, it will probably undermine any vestiges of passion. When we over-analyze others, dissecting all their behavior and motivations, we risk dehumanizing and objectifying them. Unwanted analysis creates an atmosphere of condescension.

Analysis of someone's psyche often leaves out that which is lovable and unique in a person — their ineffable essence.

Understanding the psychological dynamics in our lives can be enormously helpful and allow us to improve our lives and relationships. Yet each person has to be in charge of his or her own psychological process.

It's fine to share *our own* experiences or describe how a psychological theory has been illuminating for *us*. But rather than label our partners, children, or friends, we should attempt to see the beauty in them, even beneath the pain and the flaws. Ideally, we enrich another's life primarily by reciprocal connection and respect for each other's autonomy.

An example

Imagine that Sheila's partner Brian is frustrated with his boss. Sheila asserts that he's having a mid-life crisis and is rebelling against his boss's authority just as he rebelled against his father as a child; it is time for him to grow up. Will Brian react positively to her analysis of him? It's doubtful.

Instead, Sheila might help Brian explore his various feelings regarding the situation — if he's willing to do so, that is. She might share her experience in a similar situation or even make some suggestions, but without an attitude of expertise about his psyche, and without trying to manipulate him.

How do we know if we are alienating others?

A listener's reactions generally tell us whether we're speaking without any connection and vitality. If your listener has glazed-over eyes, you can bet that there's no linkage between you. If your listener is angry and rebellious, or cold and withdrawn, chances are you are approaching the situation with an attitude of superiority.

Some listeners simply listen and nod, which is a dynamic that may feel good to both the expert and the novice for a short while. Yet subservient adulation eventually becomes draining and tiresome for the listener, while it lacks challenge for the expert. Eventually, that sort of one-way relationship is neither satisfying nor reciprocal.

How can we effectively convey knowledge?

The most precious gift we can give another is our presence in the moment. Great communication involves keeping in touch with what is alive in us and what is alive in the other.[3] This is also known as *being* with another person and is much more appreciated than doing something to them, such as lecturing, trying to improve them, or showing off to them.

Communication from the heart is epitomized by Martin Luther King's riveting *I have a Dream* speech — a far cry from detached, dogmatic droning. The speech speaks volumes over and above the remarkable content, because the connection King has with his own heart and that of the audience is alive with nuance, energy, and passion. Although we all have our own style, some quiet and others outspoken, we can move our own mountains by keeping in touch with that which moves within us and within others.

Compassion: "How can I have compassion for someone who is angry at me?"

In their shoes

Compassion is at the very heart of good communication and a meaningful relationship. Being compassionate involves imagining being in someone else's shoes and having the desire to ease their suffering.

Suffering

Suffering often results from losing someone or something meaningful. Paradoxically, suffering is closely linked with joy because within every moment of joy lies the potential of loss. Since the hours of joy are fleeting, they are tinged with the shadow of sadness.

On the other hand, suffering also often retains elements of the joy we once experienced. Like blues music, a sweet bitterness expresses a longing for or loss of a soulful connection.

Becoming more compassionate deepens our ability to have meaningful and joyful relationships. When we become aware of the following impediments to compassion, we can open ourselves up to the ability to feel more deeply.

Compassion Impediments:

1. **Excessive judgment.** Communication without compassion imprisons us in a world of extreme judgment. Judgment uses language that implies wrongness or badness. "You're lazy." "She's selfish." "He's narcissistic." Blame, insults, and labels don't enhance life, they drain it. It's tempting and easy to judge things as good or evil, right or wrong, or black or white, but we do so out of fear or contempt. Nobody's needs, least of all our own, will be met that way.

2. **Comparison.** Comparing people to each other or ourselves can prevent us from having empathy for them. For example, comparing our own accomplishments to more accomplished people can cause us to feel thoroughly demoralized rather than inspired. However, our personal joy in life need not be compared to anyone else's.

3. **Denial of responsibility** for our actions. We all remember the Nazi system of invoking higher authority, which authorized normal people to commit horrendous crimes against humanity. When we deny responsibility for our actions, we enter dangerous territory and distance ourselves from our own humanity.

   Even if we may be tempted to say, "she makes me unhappy" or "he makes me angry," we need to take responsibility for our expectations, feelings, and actions. When we learn to handle disappointment with understanding and compassion, we are in the best position to adjust our future expectations of those who continue to disappoint us.

Compassion does not mean agreement

Compassion does not mean having to listen to endless gripes and complaints, which can be exhausting and unproductive. Compassion does not require fixing people's problems or agreeing with their thinking. We can feel compassion for someone's state of mind even if we don't agree with his or her point of view or perception.

Instead, compassion calls for giving someone our full attention and presence. Often, we can help ease someone's pain simply by witnessing and empathizing with his or her suffering.

Anger

Should we have compassion for someone who is angry at us? Absolutely, even though it may not be easy! Once we look behind the anger, we'll find the person's vulnerability, such as fear, loss, or unmet desire. Finding compassion for someone who is angry can make the difference between having painful conflict and productive communication.

For example, if your partner is angry because you're absorbed in your own activities, becoming defensive simply continues the cycle of anger. Once you see the hurt or fear driving the anger, there's a better chance of communicating effectively about what really matters to each person.

Compassion for oneself

We need to be as compassionate toward ourselves as we are toward others. Understanding the dynamic that leads us to lose our temper, for example, is more effective than harsh self-criticism. Looking for the fear or hurt beneath our own temper allows us to find a better way to address the real problem. Ruthless self-condemnation and criticism, on the other hand, simply bury the hurt or unmet need deeper until enough pressure accumulates to cause another explosion.

Compassion does not mean tolerating abuse

Boundaries are always important in any relationship. Understanding and compassion do not preclude protecting oneself from further harm. If your spouse has been violent toward you, for example, although you might try to understand how that situation developed, you should not accept the behavior or stay in a situation where it can be repeated.

Compassion recognizes the humanity in all people, and accepts that all of us have our weaknesses. Yet being compassionate does not mean condoning or tolerating abusive behavior. We can have compassion for people who have hurt us or others while still holding them accountable for their actions.

Analyzing people: "You're just re-enacting your relationship with your father!"

Telling people that they are just like their mother or re-enacting their relationship with their father is not usually helpful — even if it's true.

People don't like being analyzed, especially in a condescending way. Unless the analysis is offered with just the right intention, it feels patronizing and invasive to have someone deconstruct your behavior. Moreover, no one really knows the true motivations of another person.

Being present

Yet it can be interesting to try to make sense of people's behavior and satisfying to offer helpful insight. People who analyze others may feel closer to them when they understand their behavior.

However, focusing too much on analyzing others can lead you to miss the best part of a relationship — experiencing a deeper connection, which requires simply being present.

The time you spend with others is more meaningful and enjoyable when you feel their energetic essence. Even good therapy involves more than penetrating mental analysis. It involves a connection beyond the mind, based on an appreciation of the ineffable qualities of that particular person.

Relationships in general need to have a sense of fondness as their basis. Once a connection is forged, insightful analysis can be helpful, as long as it is welcomed. It is best offered with humility rather than certainty, and with kindness rather than condescension. But if you ever do want to tell people that they are acting just like their mother or father, do it with a sense of humor.

In some cases simply being present is all that is needed.

Peer Pressure: "That's what everyone's pushing me to do."

A person can't choose wisely for life unless he dares to listen to himself, his own self, at each moment in life.

~Abraham Maslow

When we listen primarily to others, we don't pay attention to our inner voice. To get beyond the impulse to succumb to peer pressure, we need to become self-aware. Here are five steps to enhance self-awareness:

1. Step aside and spend a few moments alone.
2. Slow down the pace of your thoughts.
3. Become more mindful of your physical and emotional state in the present moment.
4. Be aware of your tendencies and patterns of behavior, such as wanting to please or impress others.
5. Anticipate and mentally rehearse your response if you get into a situation of intense peer pressure.

Self-awareness requires listening to your thoughts and beliefs with curiosity rather than judgment.

Problems with peer pressure

1. You may find that some of your choices aimed at pleasing or impressing others may in fact not be very meaningful to those peers you are trying to please. They are often more concerned with their own image than others'.
2. You may find that going along with peer pressure comes at an unfair cost to yourself and those closest to you.
3. You may find that some of your actions directed toward avoiding pain in fact inflict greater suffering than pleasure in the long run. For example, excessive accommodation of others, busyness, and addictive behaviors are often automatic responses that harm you in the long-term.

Your own inner experience can become your best guide in how to engage with the world. When you listen to the authentic voice of your heart, you will know whether a given course of action is the one you desire or if you are simply yielding to pressure or coercion. You can also consider whether the current trajectory of your life is meaningful or whether you should take steps to change your course. With mindfulness, you can discover that a deeper sense of awareness of yourself will reward you with a deeper sense of happiness that comes from intentionally choosing to live the life you desire.

Ask yourself what makes you come alive, and go do that, because what the world needs is people who have come alive.

~Howard Thurman

Forgiveness: "I can't get over it; she really hurt me."

The weak can never forgive. Forgiveness is the attribute of the strong.

~Mahatma Gandhi

Why is it that only the strong can forgive? It may be because it is difficult to stop thinking about the unjust treatment we have received. It is also often easier to have an excuse for not living our lives to the fullest. It takes strength not to dwell on whatever unfairness does not exist among people. It takes courage to go after what we want in life and to face failure and rejection.

Resentment weakens you

Ironically, holding onto anger, no matter how justified, keeps you in victim status to the perpetrator, which results in the constriction of your heart, spirit, and mind.

Forgiveness, not approval!

Forgiveness does not mean you approve of the hurtful behavior you have received. Forgiveness does not mean forgetting. We should *learn* from the injustices done in order to avoid similar situations in the future. As a matter of fact, it is crucial to protect yourself and sometimes to protect others from similar harm. Yet learning to beware does not prevent you from also choosing to stop feeling angry toward those who have caused you harm.

Freedom

Forgiveness is not an easy or normal human reaction. But once you decide to let go of the desire to be obsessed by your anger toward someone who has hurt you, you free your heart and mind to live more expansively.

> *Forgiveness does not change the past, but it does enlarge the future.*
>
> ~Paul Boese

---

[1] Carol S. Dweck, *Mindset: The New Psychology of Success.*

[2] Drs. Hal and Sidra Stone describe the development of various "selves" or primary personality types in their "psychology of the selves," including the "expert," the "pleaser", the "responsible one."

[3] Dr. Marshall Rosenberg, who wrote "Nonviolent Communication" uses this expression: keeping in touch with what is alive in a person."

5. CONFLICT

"STOP YELLING AT ME YOU IDIOT!!"

So... what I really meant was...

"I feel very defensive when you raise your voice like that. Let's talk when we are both calm."

We're all human. Reactivity is not going to suddenly disappear. But we *can* resist continuing the blame game and we *can* become quicker at apologizing for our behavior. The sooner we take a step back to calm down or apologize for being reactive, the sooner we can get back to having a more effective conversation.

Control and Keeping Tabs: "I've texted you five times in the last hour! Where have you been?"

Keeping your partner on a short rope often results from fear of losing that person. However, the shorter the rope, the more trouble you'll have. Having a tight grip is a fast way to lose your handle on the relationship. Living in a state of paranoid obsessive possessiveness will inevitably cause a painful crash and destroy the relationship.

Obsession destroys intimacy

Checking in to say "hello" or make plans is a nice show of warmth and affection. But incessant calling or texting will spiral into an emotionally-fused relationship.

When there is too much focus on a relationship but hardly any energy is directed toward your own functioning, you can develop a need to be in constant contact simply to feel balanced.

After the initial flattery of being pursued wears off, a person under constant surveillance might start hiding perfectly innocent behavior. He or she may become annoyed and evasive, arousing further suspicion and monitoring. The relationship may become inflexible and constrained, an example of "the short-rope syndrome."

Freedom nurtures desire

The better you learn to be patient and live with your insecurity about the relationship without knee-jerk texting or calling, the more emotionally-whole and grounded you will become, and the healthier your relationship will be. When you are more whole as an individual, you're able to give your partner freedom without keeping constant tabs. Freedom and time apart are essential ingredients for a relationship based on desire and free choice.

Being Defensive: "What do you mean by that? You're always attacking me!"

It's important to be able to stand up and defend yourself. However, *defending yourself* does not mean *acting defensively*.

A defensive person is overly sensitive to criticism, anxiously trying to challenge or avoid it. The more anxiety you show in the face of criticism, the weaker your position becomes and the more criticism you invite.

Four reasons not to be defensive:

1. Defensiveness weakens you. Showing anxiety when you're criticized indicates that you buy into the attack or criticism being made. A heated response to a comment or criticism makes you look guilty or vulnerable.
2. Defensiveness empowers the hostile person. By showing your agitation, you give the assailant power over you.
3. Defensiveness creates a vicious cycle of hurt and counterattack, which puts the other person on the defensive too, leading to an escalation of personal attacks.
4. Defensive strategies hinder open communication and clear understanding between partners — the antithesis of creating goodwill and romance.

Firm not agitated

I'm not suggesting passively accepting a personal attack. You may need to establish firm boundaries, but doing so without becoming defensive will be more effective. Answering comments or criticisms with less emotional heat diminishes the likelihood of hurtful, unproductive reactions and conflict.

If your emotions are getting the better of you, you can say, "I feel defensive right now and prefer to discuss this a little later. Otherwise, nothing good will come of this discussion." Notice that *saying* you feel defensive shows more self-control than *acting* defensively.

"Why are you calling me lazy? I deserve to relax once in a while! I do more than anyone around here."

So… what I really meant was…

"It's great to relax and recharge. This is just what I need."

Own your need to relax and you will take away the potential power struggle that comes from an aggressive response.

"My ex was a psycho!"

When you tell others that your ex was a psycho, you might just as well have told them a few of the following things about *yourself*:

1. You don't take responsibility for your role in a relationship.
2. You have poor judgment in making important decisions.
3. You cause loved ones to become so angry they seem crazy.
4. You are a black-and-white thinker, and don't understand the complexity of relationships and your role in them.
5. You say bad things about those who were once closest to you.

Most ex-wives and husbands who are called "psychos" are simply regular people who feel hurt, angry, and temporarily out of control. Many people have been there to some degree.

There are occasional circumstances in which someone marries a true psychopath without knowing it. These cases are rare and you probably won't find their partners saying, "My ex was a psycho!" Their experience was just too painful to make light of the situation.

It would be more honest, thoughtful, and accountable to say something like, "We had our differences, and let our frustration get the better of us. I think we are both better off now and have learned something from the relationship."

Sounds too levelheaded? Then add, "I drove my ex crazy with my moodiness / indifference / selfishness."

> *Taking responsibility is one of the most empowering things you can do. It makes you more credible and powerful.*
>
> ~Juana Olga Maloof

Punishing Partners: "I can't stand going home after a trip because my partner punishes me for 'abandoning' him."

If your partner punishes you for going on a trip or for doing the things you love to do, it's time to set things straight — in an adult way. A loving relationship involves wanting the best for your partner as well as for yourself. This means rising above feelings of fear and possessiveness in order to support the other when he or she desires to take a trip, visit friends and family, or pursue a passion.

Often possessive behavior is a result of having felt abandoned at some time in the past. Unfortunately, the punishing partner does not realize that his or her possessiveness usually has the effect of driving the other person away, the very thing he or she is trying to prevent. It's helpful to communicate *compassionately* about your needs and desires, while still standing firm for what's important to you.

You could say something like, "I'm sorry you're sad that I went on a trip. Yet your bitterness pushes me away and causes me anguish. It's very important for me to see my family/go surfing/go to a yoga retreat. It fulfills me and revitalizes my soul. If you could be happy for me, that would deepen my appreciation and love for you. Let's both try to rise above our fears and be the best we can be to each other."

Keep in mind, it's also important to spend quality time with your partner, and not to spend *every* evening and weekend on your own.

"We always argue. Can't you just load the dishwasher this way?"

If arguments are the norm in your relationship then there is a deeper and more complex issue at play. You might think you're arguing about how to load the dishwasher (40% of couples do!) but perhaps what's really bothering you is how little appreciation you receive. You may think you're arguing about how to drive, but what you really may be upset about is not being taken seriously.

If you find yourself arguing a lot, reflect upon what it is that you are really seeking?

Examples of underlying motivations

I have to prove my point because
1. I want to feel worthwhile.
2. I want to feel understood.
3. I want to be validated.

4.   I want to improve the other person.

5.   I want to be respected.

If these motivations remain unrecognized, they can sabotage the connection between people and prevent effective communication. People often argue in an effort to coerce appreciation or respect from the other person. Yet coercive argument only results in hostility and resistance.

Effective communication

When discussing difficult issues, focus on two primary and essential motivations:

1.   to find out what the other person believes and wants, and

2.   to express yourself in a way that the other person will hear you without becoming defensive.

To communicate effectively and avoid bitter arguments, try the following:

1.   Listen more and really try to understand what the other person thinks and feels. Put yourself in his or her shoes.

2.   Let the other person finish his or her thoughts before expressing another point of view.

3.   Use a neutral tone of voice and body language to avoid triggering the other person.

4.   Express, rather than hide, opinions and desires that are important to you.

5.   Be ready to simply accept your differences.

Relationships improve when people can discuss their true opinions and desires both passionately *and* compassionately. When you are motivated to enhance your relationship by respecting the other person, communication becomes more effective and pleasant.

Talk about the real issue, and then settle on a compromise about how to load the dishwasher. In the scheme of life that kind minor difference of opinion is not worth a power struggle.

"Anger is unhealthy and bad."

Anybody can become angry — that is easy, but to be angry with the right person and to the right degree and at the right time and for the right purpose, and in the right way — that is not within everybody's power and is not easy.

~Aristotle

Anger is a signal

Anger in a relationship is *usually* a healthy reaction to current or feared mistreatment, including being hurt, overlooked, or betrayed. Anger is a helpful emotion because it makes us aware of possible unfairness or maltreatment. It can appropriately signify that an injustice has been done or is occurring.

Thus, we don't want to eliminate or repress anger. What's key is how we respond to anger. We need to take note of it and inquire into the real causes of the perceived injustice without jumping to conclusions or reacting too heatedly.

Ongoing rage

Ongoing rage, as opposed to anger, is often exhibited by people who are ineffective, unaccountable, or powerless. People who storm around, rage, and point fingers don't take responsibility for themselves and are ineffective in improving their situation and their own lives.

Anger as your ally

Anger, however, is a necessary emotion signaling to us to take a look at our circumstances to see if an injustice is occurring. Here's how we make anger our ally:

1. Be accountable

a. Change your interaction

One of the keys to making anger your ally is to develop the habit of clarifying how much *you yourself* may be contributing to the unfairness or offense. For instance, you may be contributing by provoking someone with veiled insults, a condescending attitude, or simply by continuing to accept mistreatment as it gradually worsens. When you know if and how you are contributing to the problem, you can change your role in the interaction.

b. Subdue the inner drama

When you become more accountable for your own participation in a given problem or situation, bitterness tends to diminish. Remain self-aware while you are angry, and you may hear an inner voice say, "you're overreacting; you'll have to be accountable for this," or "you're staying in this unworkable situation; you'll have to get out of it." Knowing that if you lose your temper you will have to be accountable by apologizing or taking action tends to subdue the inner drama.

c. Don't put others on the defensive

When you respond to your anger without adding to the conflict with attacks and hostility, you can prevent a situation from escalating out of control.

When intimates know that you will eventually take responsibility for your part in a confrontation, whether that occurs in five minutes or three days, heated exchanges tend to be less acrimonious. The fact that others know that you will be accountable and hold them accountable causes everyone to be more circumspect.

2. Look at all sides

People who are angry cannot experience empathy. On the other hand, if you are determined to empathize with another person, despite how demanding that can be, it's difficult to remain angry.

Learning to see the situation from the other person's perspective softens the intensity of anger and informs you how to communicate more effectively with that person. When you learn to look at several perspectives at once, rather than being locked into your own perspective, your anger softens, and so will your self-righteousness.

3. Take action

By understanding the other person's perspective, you'll be able to focus on taking effective action, which is where the real power lies. Mistreatment requires meaningful action. Anger should be viewed as a signal that everything is not as it should be. The key is to remain in control in order to figure out an effective way to handle the situation.

"Why does my partner criticize me all the time? I'm never good enough."

Some people tend to be critical of others, while others tend to be more critical of themselves. Often these contrasting types of people are drawn to one another because they each need to develop a moderate dose of the opposite quality. When one partner tends to criticize the other partner all the time, both partners are partaking in the underlying dynamic, which means that either partner can do something to change it.

Self-critical people

People who have been severely criticized while growing up often develop an excessively harsh inner critic to stop themselves from doing something wrong before the other person catches them. Moderate self-criticism is a good thing, as it leads to self-awareness and allows a person to see where there's room for self-improvement.

However, overly self-critical people are primed to expect and even trigger criticism, as they are the first to see their own flaws — real or imagined. By their unconscious self-criticism, they invite others to see them the way they see themselves. If they assume they are awkward or unintelligent, for example, they express those attitudes toward themselves with their facial expressions and body language. Not only do they *expect* others to be critical of them, they tend to endure criticism no matter how inappropriate or harsh.

Critical people

Extremely critical people project their feelings of discomfort onto the world around them. A moderate dose of criticism, also known as discernment, enables a person to improve the world and people around them. Excessively critical people, however, become expert at finding flaws in others, which hurts them, causes them to shut down, and deadens the vitality in a relationship.

Polarization

In the beginning couples are not polarized into critical and self-critical extremes. The critical partner might simply share observations and insights in an attempt to improve life while the self-critical partner might enjoy receiving helpful suggestions.

Eventually, however, excessive criticism creates ongoing tension and one-sidedness in the relationship resulting in distress and heartache.

Moderating the inner critic

In order to stop putting up with excessive or destructive criticism from others, you must come to terms with your own inner critic. Ideally you want to manage your own inner judge so that it becomes a source of inspiration — supporting and encouraging your inner beauty and strength. You do this by transforming each negative self-critical thought into a constructive, helpful thought.

For example, "I'm an idiot on this tennis court," becomes "I just need to remember to bend my knees." "I look like an outsider," becomes "Who cares what I'm wearing, I'm going to enjoy this experience."

Moderating the external critic

You need to become aware of what is inappropriate or excessive criticism from others. Then you must find a way of ignoring the criticism, speaking up against it, or finding a humorous way to deflect it. The main thing is not to encourage criticism from others by being overly reactive or sullenly acquiescent.

Don't be afraid to criticize the critic. "You may not realize it, but you criticize me many times a day, and it pushes me away from you. No one is perfect, including you. Please try to improve yourself instead of me. I would appreciate it if you point out the good in me rather than the flaws."

If all else fails, try to avoid spending time with people who are excessively critical.

"My negative emotions get me down. I tend to dwell on feeling hurt or angry."

Life is like riding a bicycle. To keep your balance you must keep moving.

~Albert Einstein

Responding to negative emotions

Negative emotions often indicate that what we are doing is not working for us. They often provide a signal that we need to become more flexible, that is, that we need to change our perceptions, our expectations, and/or our actions.

Flexibility allows us to deal with whatever life hands us without lingering in pain and suffering more than necessary. By becoming more versatile, we can view the twists and turns in our lives as an adventure. That's not to say that we won't experience some losses and disappointments that will be extremely painful. Yet many losses and disappointments can be seen as signals to make necessary changes that will provide more depth and meaning to our lives.

Travel as a metaphor

Notice how adaptable some people are who enjoy traveling. They can go with the flow or change plans if necessary. If something unexpected happens, they don't say, "The train wasn't supposed to break down in the middle of nowhere on my trip to Spain." They become alert and alive, generally welcoming the adventure unfolding before them. Often the most interesting and funny stories come about through unforeseen mishaps and adversity.

Like travel, life is a journey full of surprises, adventure and disappointments. The more quickly we can respond and learn

147

from the vagaries and disappointments in life the better and richer our lives will become. Let surprising circumstances bring out the hero in you, not the victim. When the unexpected occurs, ask yourself, "How can I view this as an adventure?"

Misunderstandings

Misunderstandings in relationships are like unexpected mishaps while traveling. They give rise to an opportunity to make the best of the situation and bring about greater understanding.

When you feel misunderstood, ask yourself, "Why would that person have understood me that way? How is he/she viewing the situation?"

When you feel hurt, ask yourself, "How can I change my expectations of the person who has hurt me?"

When you are angry, ask yourself, "What steps can I take to find justice or to avoid that same injustice in the future?"

Life is pretty simple: You do some stuff. Most fails. Some works. You do more of what works. If it works big, others quickly copy it. Then you do something else. The trick is the doing something else.

~Leonardo da Vinci

"She's just like my mother! — so weak!"
"He's just like my father — so controlling!"

The quality of all of our relationships is a direct function of our relationship to ourselves.

~James Hollis

Just like my mother/father

No one influences our relationship to ourselves as much as our parents or caretakers. As a result, we are sometimes drawn to people who have some of their same key qualities. While at first familiar and comforting, eventually some of those qualities can become all-too-familiar triggers to our childhood responses. For example, what at first seemed attractive — *strong and in control* — turns into *controlling and dictatorial.*

Carl Jung recognized that such projection causes much unnecessary suffering in relationships. "How many marriages are wrecked for years, and sometimes forever, because he sees his mother in his wife and she her father in her husband, and neither ever recognizes the other's reality!"[1]

The opposite of my mother/father

Some people are so annoyed by their parents that they consciously choose someone with opposite qualities. For instance, someone with a passive parent is drawn to someone who is in control.

The problem is that any quality taken to its extreme starts to resemble its opposite. For example, a controlling person tries to manage anxiety by managing another person, while a passive person may try to manage anxiety by accommodating other people. Neither is capable of independently managing his or her own anxiety.

Those who marry someone who is the opposite of one of their parents often end up experiencing unexpectedly similar dynamics as they experienced with that parent. To avoid repeating the patterns of our childhood relationship to our parents, we must learn to balance the opposite extremes of a quality and consciously choose whatever middle ground is appropriate in a given situation.

Controlling husband/wife and passive wife/husband

Imagine a wife projecting onto her husband, "You're just like my father — controlling and dictatorial." Naturally, she would respond with the same defenses as she did as a child, such as, hostility, reluctant compliance, or angry withdrawal. Any of these responses would intensify the dynamic of control between the couple. He would see her as weak and become even more domineering as a defense against vulnerability.

It is a vicious cycle that is difficult to reverse.

Projection

Projection triggers people's automatic responses and ruins their opportunity to relate in a fresh way in current situations.

By projecting all the control onto her husband, the wife disowns her personal authority, giving away the power that she could develop within herself. The husband projects away his vulnerability and becomes increasingly forceful to repress any uncomfortable feelings of uncertainty. Neither develops the ability to handle anxiety and stress, which are inevitable in life.

Taking back your projections

To avoid this unhappy cycle, the partners should try to take back their projections and overcome their automatic reactions.

For example, if you project control and authority onto your partner, you would need to develop a moderate dose of control and authority over your own life. If you project weakness and passivity onto your partner, you would need to develop sensitivity to your own feelings and vulnerabilities, and allow others to take control of their lives and make their own decisions. By taking back your projections, you gain the opportunity both to grow and to relate to your partner in a fair-minded manner.

In summary, here are the steps involved in dealing with a partner whom you view as controlling or weak:

Controlling partner

If you see your partner as controlling, you must

1.   Learn to deal effectively with controlling people,

2. Develop more personal authority to become less of a victim, and

3. Deflate the power of controlling behavior by seeing the fear of vulnerability beneath the controlling behavior.

Weak partner

If you see your partner as weak, you must

1. Learn to deal effectively with weak or passive people by being less domineering and by engaging *their* sense of self empowerment,

2. Learn to mitigate your desire to control everything,

3. Develop more sensitivity to your own weaknesses, and

4. Accept people's separateness and autonomy.

Negative Projection: "It's because of him that I never had children, and now it's too late."

It was Carl Jung who stated that thoughts and fears that remain unconscious get projected onto others. People tend to project qualities that are incompatible with their own self-image.

For instance, a wife blames her husband for their decision not to have children. Yet she may be disowning her inner desire not to have children and project it onto her husband. She may not consciously like the fact that she fears the responsibilities involved in having children, and thus repress such thoughts. Because her conscious mind finds such thoughts unacceptable, she may be unaware that she is conveniently casting such feelings onto her husband.

Here are some other examples of negative projection:

- A person who sees himself as kind and generous might not want to acknowledge even the slightest inclination toward greed, and consequently sees it only in others.

- A person blames his or her partner for having given up dreams of sailing the Caribbean, unaware of his or her hidden desire for the security of a stable job, lifestyle, and home life.

Giving away responsibility

When we have negative projections, we rarely recognize the seeds of those qualities in ourselves. Painful or incompatible qualities get projected onto another person, and that person ends up becoming the target of our anger or contempt.

For example, by projecting onto your husband the decision not to have children, you disown your own free will. You disregard your own part in that decision. Ultimately, *you* made the choice not to have children. You could have talked your partner into it, discussed it before getting together, or left him rather than abiding by his preference. You *chose* to stay with him and agreed to his preference not to have children.

Taking responsibility for our decisions (or lack thereof)

In the quest for wholeness, our task is to take back our projections. By taking back the responsibility for making our own decisions, we become aware of our true priorities and choices. When we stop blaming others, we gain freedom and control in our lives. There will still be losses and compromises, but we will no longer live with resentment toward others, which is one of the keys to sustaining fulfilling long-term relationships.

"I feel miserable, stifled, and as though I don't exist in this relationship. I have to move out, but don't want to hurt him."

It's always worthwhile to avoid unnecessarily hurting another person. However, feeling miserable and stifled is detrimental not only for your psyche and health, but for your partner and your relationship as well.

In limbo

Not making a decision is a decision in itself, which may be damaging for both of you.

If you are absolutely clear that you need to break up, the sooner you do so, the more time both of you will have to rebuild your lives. Staying with someone without a mutual commitment to enhance your relationship hurts both of you.

Remaining in a state of limbo causes your partner to hold out hope (indeed your partner may be completely unaware of your feelings) and prevents both of you from addressing the problem or moving on with your lives.

Kind but clear

We all need to balance taking care of ourselves with making others happy. When you ignore what is important for you to the point that you are miserable, you endanger your health and wellbeing. Consideration for others is commendable, but one must be able to say "No" and "Enough" when appropriate.

Now is your chance to grow by taking your own needs to heart and taking appropriate action. If he cares for you he will want you to do what is best for you.

You will probably hurt him less in the long run by deciding on clear closure and giving him freedom. Treat your partner with

153

kindness and compassion. But use your personal authority and be decisive, saying something like, "I need to move out and gain back my sense of self, which I cannot do while I'm with you. It's not fair to you to live with someone who is miserable and has neither passion nor vitality. I care about you and want you to move on with your life. I have to move on with mine."

You need to be firm in bringing closure for your sake and his. It is in nobody's best interest to remain in a relationship that is causing one person to be miserable and stifled.

"People are always criticizing me."

If you are frequently criticized for a particular trait, consider whether there's a good reason for it. For example, if everyone says you talk too much, then perhaps you may want to focus on listening more.

If, however, people generally tend to openly criticize you, then you may want to consider whether your personal demeanor triggers people's critical side.

Body language — anticipating criticism

As we grow up, we learn to anticipate how people are going to treat us before we actually interact. That anticipation makes it more likely that our interactions will go the way we expect. Our facial expressions and body language convey our expectations, and people tend to respond as we expect them to.

If you are used to being criticized, you anticipate feeling hurt and dejected. Just before an interaction, you may slightly cringe, look down, or appear unsure. When people subliminally notice body language that conveys dejection, it often brings out their critical side, just as weakness tends to attract bullies. Body language that conveys insecurity triggers criticism in others.

Change your body language

Facial expressions that convey confidence and anticipate acceptance tend to induce a favorable response.

It may be time to purposely change your expectations and your corresponding body language. At first, you can simply pretend that you expect to be accepted and appreciated, rather than criticized. In other words, when you approach others, anticipate the positive. Once people start responding more positively, you'll no longer need to pretend to expect the best. It will come naturally.

"I can't deal with my husband's anger. Even if his anger is about work, I leave the room."

Say something before walking away

If you can't handle being in the room when someone's angry, then leaving might be necessary and the appropriate response. But try not to walk away without a brief explanation.

It's important to let the person know that although his anger may be justified, the way he expresses his anger makes you feel apprehensive and upset. Explain that you feel overwhelmed by the force of his energy and volume of his voice, even though you know he's not angry at you. Tell him that you want to hear what's going on in his life at work when he calms down.

Too sensitive?

It's also important to consider whether you are perhaps overly sensitive to any display of anger, in which case you might want to work on thickening your skin and becoming more resilient. If you allow a few minutes of venting, his anger is likely to diminish.

Compassion for anger?

Should you have compassion for someone who is angry? Absolutely, even though it may not be easy. Try to see through the anger to the underlying hurt or fear that's fueling that anger. When you see the vulnerability underneath, it's much harder to take anger personally, even when it is aimed at you.

"I get enraged when she lies to me."

Lying may have its place in certain situations

Imagine being a Jew in Germany during WW II. It would be extremely risky to admit this fact to a Nazi. Who among us would not lie if the potential consequences of telling the truth were deadly.

This is an extreme example, but we can take it down dramatically. People often learn to distort or hide the truth when they fear either dire consequences, an overreaction, or imminent pain. A person may have grown up in an environment where an angry or cold parent seemed dangerous to the psyche's very existence. Thus many people start lying in order to avoid the overreaction of their family of origin.

Motivation for lying

People learn to react to emotionally-dangerous circumstances in different ways, including being rebellious, disappearing emotionally, and being compliant. Part of being compliant is adapting to what we think the other person wants in order to avoid arousing an adverse reaction. A compliant person might hide or distort the truth in order to avoid confrontation, to gain connection, or to keep the peace.

Transform fury into fair-mindedness

You won't stop others from lying by pounding your fist on the table or by seething with anger. You'll just cause them to withdraw and become better liars.

So if your family members hide the truth or lie to you in order to please or appease you, it's worthwhile to consider whether your reaction to their behavior have something to do with it. Ask yourself whether you tend to react with too much drama, criticism, or hostility instead of logical consequences. Ask yourself whether you can handle the truth.

Although you can't ensure that others will be honest, you can promote their honesty by being compassionate and reasonable. This doesn't mean that there shouldn't be consequences for bad behavior. But if you respond with a fair-minded discussion and respond appropriately, people will be more willing to be honest with you.

"I've been physically and emotionally abused. Why do I stay?"

Long-term emotional or physical abuse often causes progressively more agonizing suffering and can even become life-threatening. There is no excuse for physical abuse or ongoing emotional abuse. It is imperative to remove yourself quickly from a situation of abuse, because it becomes increasingly difficult to leave an abusive relationship as your self-esteem worsens and you become more isolated.

Why do people stay? When people lose strong connections to family, friends, and outside community, they feel emotionally attached to their partners despite the obvious abuse. Others feel so poorly about themselves that they seem unable to imagine a different future or to feel worthy of respect and consideration. Some get lost in a world of trying to defend themselves or of behaving "perfectly" to avoid further abuse. Many others feel trapped by their financial situation and dependence.

Rebuilding one's soul requires finding safe shelter. Only by being away from the emotional and physical abuse can one experience the freedom from fear to think about one's own needs and desires, as well as to regain self-respect necessary to gain authority over one's own life.

While most physical abuse is against women, there is plenty of physical and emotional abuse against men as well. In either case, finding friends or shelter away from the abuser is the best way to develop the strength, sense of self, and self-respect in order to seek an abuse-free life again.

Although a shelter for abused women is not a vacation spot — it has to have rules and conditions to thrive, as well as to foster accountability and community — it is a safe place to go that allows women to get counseling, rebuild their lives, their self-esteem, and their sense of peace. It is a place where they can learn how to effectively respond to disrespectful behavior long before it reaches levels of abuse.

Anybody who experiences ongoing contempt or abuse must find a way to separate him- or herself from the abusive person. It is very difficult to lead the best life you can when you live in an atmosphere that is psychologically oppressing or outright dangerous. Ideally, you would want to be among people who are loving, supportive, and encouraging. At a minimum, a neutral, peaceful environment allows you the freedom to gain perspective about yourself and to develop the necessary boundaries and self-respect to live the life you desire.

---

[1] Jung, C.G., *The practice of psychotherapy*. p. 219.

6. INTIMACY

"You never kiss me anymore."

Many couples gradually stop kissing over time. This can be a sign that they no longer cherish one another — the result of an insidious invasion of indifference or resentment into the relationship.

First wait for the right situation and try enticing your partner to kiss you. Don't complain or whine, but say something like, "I love kissing you," and try seducing your partner into a kiss. See the movie "Hitch" for a great scene about kissing.

Candid communication

If that doesn't work, it's important to have frank conversations about changes in your relationship that bother you. The situation is not going to improve without your broaching the subject.

If you want the truth, don't get angry or anticipate feeling hurt. Be direct, but set the stage so that your partner won't feel attacked. You could say something like, "I want to be in a relationship where there's mutual affection and intimacy. I'd like to know why you don't kiss me/show affection/make love to me anymore."

Be ready for an honest response. Hopefully, it's something easy to deal with — maybe you have bad breath, in which case it's easy to talk to a dentist or doctor. Maybe your partner didn't even notice the gradual erosion of intimacy that has occurred and just needed a reminder.

Causes of lack of desire

It could be something more serious, such as lack of desire and attraction. Many things can lead to lack of desire. Here are three main areas to consider:

1. **Resentment.** People stop being affectionate when they feel resentment, which can result from feeling taken for granted, treated as secondary, controlled, or criticized. Ask whether your attitude toward your partner is causing him or her to withdraw affection and openness.

2. **Lack of self-respect or self-care.** People may also lose interest when their partners let themselves go, living in such a way that shows they've lost respect for themselves. When people don't have the discipline or motivation to take care of themselves physically, intellectually, and emotionally, their partners generally lose desire for them. Ask yourself whether your attitude toward yourself is inviting desire. We're not talking about getting face lifts and liposuction, but simply maintaining a healthy lifestyle and vibrancy about yourself.

3. **Lack of sensuality or presence.** Kissing may come to an end because it is too mechanical, lackluster, or insensitive. This might reflect one's attitude toward oneself or the other person or it might be the result of not being tuned in with one's sensuality.

Intent, appreciation, passion

Some people view kissing to be just about the most intimate physical contact, revealing a person's true sensuality and interest. In good kissing, like in good relationships, there's a balance in the enjoyment of giving and receiving. Curiosity and desire are focused on the person being kissed.

Positive Bonding Patterns: "We don't fight, but there's not much passion or conversation anymore."

Love, but not *in love*

How often have you heard people say, "I still love him/her, but I'm not in love anymore"? This loss of passion is often the result of falling into what Drs. Hal and Sidra Stone call a "positive bonding pattern"[1] through countless decisions to hide true opinions and feelings in order to appease the other person.

Positive bonding patterns feel good at first because they are comfortable and safe. Yet ironically they are detrimental to the long-term health of a relationship. Each person puts on an attitude of agreement to placate the other and to avoid bringing up painful points of view or differing opinions. Each accommodates the other beyond the point of reasonable compromise.

Don't rock the boat

Positive bonding patterns usually occur because we don't want to rock the boat. Anxious to avoid upsetting the other person, we keep difficult thoughts and feelings to ourselves and put on a happy face.

However, thoughts and feelings that are hidden in a relationship will grow and fester. Eventually, the positive bonding pattern will lead to a lifeless relationship or a negative bonding pattern, in which fighting, anger, and bitterness will consume the relationship.

Examples

A woman doesn't like the way her partner touches her physically, but she never says anything about it. As a consequence, the physical relationship is likely to peter out. She might remain agreeable, but she will find ways of avoiding physical intimacy.

Likewise, a man who never reveals that he dislikes the way his partner treats him may suddenly leave the relationship after years of acquiescence in search of the dignity and respect he craves.

If a partner does not express his or her differing opinions, discussions are likely to become dull and one-sided, and eventually come to an end. Silent judgments intensify. The relationship becomes stagnant and predictable. Sexual intimacy loses its passion or disappears.

When your opinions and preferences go underground, you lose your passion for life, and ultimately, your sense of self.

Ways to avoid a positive bonding pattern:

1. Learn to communicate effectively, so that you can be honest without being hostile.

2. Avoid pretending to think or feel something that you don't in order to keep the peace. You're less likely to develop underground judgments and resentments.

3. Resist becoming overly dependent on another person, and you'll feel less need to mollify that him or her.

4. Minimize overreacting, manipulating, and controlling your partner into doing what you want and agreeing with you. Then it will be easier for your partner to retain a sense of self, which is vital for sustaining a long-term passionate relationship.

Contempt: *"Don't look at me that way!"*

Contempt destroys relationships

Studies have shown that people who make sour facial expressions when their spouses talk are likely to be separated within four years.[2] Contempt expresses disdain, loathing, and disrespect.

Contempt breaks the heart. It eats away at a relationship rapidly and painfully. In an atmosphere of contempt, partners find it difficult to remember anything positive about the other.

Breaking the cycle

It's very important to break this cycle before it gets a stranglehold on the relationship. In a loving but firm way, express your desire and need to be treated with love and respect. Say something like, "You may not be aware of this or mean anything by it, but you look as though you dislike me. Your facial expression puts me on the defensive."

If your partner doesn't get it, show him or her the research on relationships and contempt. Google "contempt in marriage" or get any of John Gottman's books, such as "The Seven Principles for Making Marriage Work."

Most importantly, if your partner knows that you have the desire and courage to make the choices necessary to be treated well, you will retain power over your own life and the trajectory of the relationship. If you're determined not to let contemptuous behavior slide, your partner will be hard pressed to have contempt for you. But if the behavior continues despite ongoing efforts, the only solution may be to terminate the relationship.

"Why can't we spend more time together? You always need more space!"

Emotional cat and mouse.

The ability to have a passionate, fulfilling relationship requires that a couple balance two primary drives — intimacy and independence. If you don't consciously balance these needs, you may wind up in the frustrating dynamic of the *Pursuer* and the *Distancer*. Pursuers pursue intimacy, unaware of their need for autonomy. Distancers seek autonomy, unaware of their need for intimacy.

The Pursuer/Distancer Dynamic

People who seek more connection — or *Pursuers* — tend to say things like, "Let's talk," or "What are you thinking about?" They like sharing thoughts and feelings, and feel personally rejected when their partner needs some space. As a result, they try harder. Eventually they start a fight or withdraw angrily attempting to create connection by provoking the Distancer's anger or fear.

People who keep physical or emotional distance — or *Distancers* — enjoy independence and autonomy. They tend to be self-reliant and have difficulty showing vulnerability. They manage their personal relationships by intensifying work, activities outside the relationship, or brooding alone. When a relationship becomes too difficult, they tend to end it abruptly.

Evolution of Pursuer/Distancer Dynamic

We tend to attract into our lives people with characteristics that we have unconsciously disowned. That's why Distancers and Pursuers frequently get into relationships with one another. They each need to develop a bit of the opposite quality to balance their one-sidedness.

Pursuers feel that the connection they received in childhood did not adequately satisfy their need to be seen or loved, and thus they spend their adulthood pursuing connection. They are often attracted to strong independent types. They tend to seek connection with a subconscious fear and expectation of being disappointed, which eventually comes across as needy and undesirable. As a result, their craving for connection often backfires. Thus, the cycle of near connection and rejection continues.

Distancers may have been left to themselves in their childhood, lived in a chaotic environment, or have been hurt deeply at some point. As a way to protect themselves, they become very independent. They are often attracted to those who tend to be pursuers. Otherwise, how would a Distancer get together with anyone?

As the relationship develops, Distancers often feel smothered by the pursuers' attention and desire for more connection. Based on their history they may feel they have good reason to fear that intimacy is likely to lead to dependence, constraint, or disappointment. Their partner's apparent intrusiveness leads them to dread exposing their own vulnerabilities. As a result, they seek space and solitude.

How do People become Pursuers or Distancers?

Imagine a boy falling down and crying, "I'm bleeding!" The natural reaction of the parent is either to get upset with his outburst and reprimand, "Stop crying!" or to run over anxiously to help him. A more effective response would be in the middle-ground, remaining calm and saying something like "Yes, blood ... Let's take a look at it and wash it." This validates the child's reaction, while moving him or her to a calmer place. Thus, the child learns how to stay calm in moments of high anxiety.

Responding to a child's needs without becoming too anxious is what Donald Winnicott referred to as "good-enough mothering." "Good-enough parenting" allows a child to learn to stay calm without developing dread of being smothered, alienated, or infantilized.

Yet how many of us are ideal parents or had ideal parents? If during anxious moments as an infant we were neglected or smothered with attention or some sort of heated reaction, subsequent situations of too much separateness or too much togetherness may cause us to experience inappropriately high anxiety.

The perception of too much separateness can trigger feelings of being neglected, abandoned, unloved, and rejected. The perception of too much togetherness can activate feelings of being crowded, trapped, and controlled.

Self-defeating behavior

Later in life, Distancers often avoid saying what they think in order to avoid escalating anxiety. Pursuers may then feel ignored and try to get a reaction to make a connection, which increases the stress for both of them.

Thus the Pursuer/Distancer dynamic often leads to hostility and argument. The person pushing for a response is seeking connection. Focusing on the other person through argument provides at least some emotional contact, albeit negative. The Distancer, who likes his or her autonomy, will resist and become hostile to protect his or her separateness and independence.

Without realizing it, the Pursuer expresses enough desire for intimacy for both partners. Therefore, the Distancer doesn't have to recognize his or her own desire for connection. If one person is doing all the pursuing, the other has the luxury to experience a need for space and independence. In fact, the Distancer may fall out of love, because there is not enough room for him or her to experience a sense of desire.

Similarly, the Distancer creates enough distance for both partners so that the Pursuer never gets a chance to recognize his or her own need for autonomy. Consequently, the Pursuer can disown any desire for autonomy. Without some sense of being a separate, capable individual, he or she feels an increasing need to be connected to his or her partner in order to feel worthwhile, furthering the vicious cycle.

Recognizing both needs

Comparable to the concept of *Yin-Yang*, intimacy and independence require each other to make a whole. Each partner needs to be able to be alone *and* to connect with others. When you become conscious of the necessity of satisfying both needs, you can seek a balance openly and avoid much pain and frustration. The result is real autonomy that allows for no-strings-attached intimacy.

Solutions for the Pursuer

The Pursuer needs to draw back and put more energy into her own life and her own separate interests. A couple who came to see me had been caught in a cycle of emotional pursuit and distancing that had escalated ever since the birth of their children. When John came home from work and retreated to his computer, Eve generally reproached him because she wanted to spend time with him.

However, when she reframed the situation in her own mind, she was able to break out of the vicious cycle. *I've been wanting him to provide me with something that I realize I need to provide for myself. I recognize that I need to do something about fulfilling my own needs.* She then rearranged her schedule so that she could take a class, get a job, and/or see friends more often.

She soon realized that some independence and space of her own choosing would enrich her life. Dropping her neediness also allowed John to feel enough separation that he started to desire her again.

Solutions for the Distancer

The Distancer has a sense of power in the relationship, because he or she has the choice as to whether or not to submit to the Pursuer's desire for connection. Yet by holding such power and fostering fear and weakness in his or her partner, the Distancer loses the opportunity to have a more fulfilling relationship.

If the Distancer needs space before talking about a subject, he or she can say "I just need some time to think. Let's talk tonight after dinner." The Distancer should then approach the Pursuer rather than waiting for the Pursuer's inevitable approach so the Pursuer is not left hanging and wondering when and if there will ever be any connection.

The Distancer needs to purposely schedule time for making emotional contact. If the Pursuer knows *when* there will be time together, it will be easier for him or her to back off pursuit of connection. It may be awkward for the Distancer to seek emotional contact with someone who is always pushing for it. But if the plan includes time for separateness, over time the practice will become habitual and less awkward.

Making the attempt to connect may actually bring balance to the relationship, by quelling the Pursuer's need to pressure the Distancer for more attention. If nothing else, it'll be worth seeing the look of surprise on his or her face!

An Example

A woman felt suffocated by what she viewed as her husband's neediness and had been running away from any contact with him.

After some discussion and thought, she decided she would make an effort to connect with him to see if things would improve. She discussed with him the idea of sitting down to dinner together five nights a week without technological devices and spending one afternoon on the weekend doing something together.

Within two days, the oppression she had been feeling lifted. Her husband hadn't wanted to spend every minute with her. He had only pursued her so unrelentingly, because she gave nothing of herself to him. Once he knew they would be connected every day, even though it was relatively brief, he stopped pestering her. In addition, he felt better about himself and became more attractive to her, because he became more calm and confident and less desperate.

Over time, the necessity to schedule time together diminished, as both partners became aware of their individual needs. Both individuals were able to find their own balance between solitude and connection within themselves.

We can purposely dance the dance of togetherness by desiring the other from a place of fullness rather than need. If you're the Pursuer, be the flame and not the moth. If you're the Distancer, try exercising your own wings.

Boundaries: "Hey, how's your dinner?" — Jab of the fork.

Romantic?

When you take a bite of your partner's food without asking, you are crossing a boundary. That kind of intimacy seems romantic to many, but over the long run the underlying assumption of entitlement can kill passion and your relationship.

Often people think that sharing food without asking is a sign of intimacy and a perk of a loving relationship. Actually, the opposite is likely to transpire. If you don't both ask *and* wait for your partner's consent, you are crossing a boundary and showing disrespect.

You might think, "We're so close that I don't need to ask — what's his or hers is mine." Yet if there's not enough separation and respect for a partner's space, including his or her food, he or she will eventually feel impinged upon and resent you for it.

It's these small, hardly noticeable infractions of respect that build up into passive aggressive responses and a yearning for freedom and space.

Beware of basic instincts

It is a basic instinct to be possessive over food and belongings. One of the first things a child learns to say is, "This is mine. Don't touch it."

So when someone reaches across the table to take your food, you will unconsciously have a protective reaction and take offense. The voice of the unconscious will say, "Get away from my food," though the conscious mind tries to rationalize, "We're close, it's okay."

If someone asks, "May I have a bite?" then we know the request is limited, and that we still have control over our food, which appeases our inner lion. We don't feel taken for granted, and we have the opportunity to feel generous by saying, "Yes, try a bite."

Ironically, respecting others' boundaries preserves the passion of a relationship, while excessive closeness and possessiveness are a sure way to kill it.

Platonic Marriage: "Once you've had children, romantic intimacy is not so important anymore."

So what I really meant was…

"A long-term *passionate* marriage is more enjoyable and fulfilling than a *platonic* one. Our relationship and lives will be richer if we keep the passion and sensuality alive."

If your partner doesn't realize how important romantic intimacy is to sustaining a long-term passionate marriage, it's vital that you have frank discussions about it together. Let your partner know that it's important to you to be in a relationship with someone who desires you and who wants to continue to have a passionate relationship.

People who go after what they want with confidence — without begging, complaining, or making threats — are far more desirable than those who extinguish their desires. If, however, your long-term partner is not interested in cultivating intimacy with you any longer, then you may have come to a crossroad in your relationship.

Intimacy: "I want more intimacy, validation, and to feel closer to you."

Some people claim they want more intimacy in their primary relationship. Yet what they really want is total compliance and validation, which are antithetical to intimacy. Long-term, passionate intimacy requires that two people have a strong enough sense of self that they can have differing opinions and preferences without expecting all-encompassing closeness, validation and accommodation from each other.

Intimacy based on accommodation

People often find it uncomfortable to deal with their partner's insecurities. It is easier to simply appease them, agree with them, and validate them. Thus, people often validate their partners simply to accommodate their fears and insecurities. Often, however, it is actually *their own anxiety* that they cannot tolerate when their partner is under stress.

For example, one may choose to respond by nodding and smiling rather than saying, "Here is another way to handle the situation, which I think would be a lot more effective."

Over the long-term validation to appease one's partner has a tremendous cost. The result of repeatedly hiding one's true thoughts is a deadening of the soul, growing resentment, and a loss of passion within the relationship.

Codependence

Validating your partner *can* temporarily improve your partner's mood and functioning. However, inauthentic validation often creates long-term problems, such as greater codependency. When couples become codependent, their vulnerability to their partner's manipulation gets magnified. Each partner will feel increasingly burdened by an obligation to ease the other person's anxiety. They feel constrained to say and do whatever will get a positive reaction from their partner. Ultimately, codependency intensifies anxiety while killing the passion, creativity, and spontaneity in the relationship.

Intimacy based on candor

True intimacy evolves when you don't manipulate your partner to validate you. When you don't need your partner to accommodate your insecurities, you can reveal parts of yourself that he or she may not agree with or validate. The benefit is that your partner then truly sees you without feeling an obligation to shore up your insecurities.

It requires confidence and courage to accept your partner's authentic response.

While it's nice to be validated by others, you are more likely to get true and meaningful validation if you don't seek it. Also differences are what create the spark necessary for passion, growth and curiosity. When you're willing to accept a person's honest response, then you can meet that person on a deeper, more intimate level. Ironically, less validation means greater intimacy and the possibility of a long-term passionate relationship.

In essence, a successful, long-term passionate relationship requires that two people have a strong enough sense of themselves that they can stand being with someone who has different ideas, tastes, and opinions.[3]

"Our relationship is such hard work. The spark is gone."

The best long-term relationships are both firmly grounded *and* light-hearted. Committed relationships, which are based on shared values and loyalty, need fleeting moments of enjoyment to carry them through the difficult times of life.

While it's important to discuss long-term goals and significant issues, it's equally important to have fun and relax together on a daily basis.

When one partner continuously wants to engage in heavy and serious discussions — about relationship issues or practical matters, the personal light-hearted part of the relationship suffers.

173

As a result, many couples stop being intimate and even stop looking at each other much or confiding in one another.

Listening to music, dancing, laughing, watching sports together, and having romantic meals are all ways to keep the personal energetic connection alive.

"After multiple affairs, he promised he'd never cheat on me again. Can I trust him this time?"

Vicious cycle

No. Sorry to say, someone who repeatedly cheats on his or her partner is unlikely to stop.

Repeated cheating usually stems from a craving for the brief psychological validation and dopamine high that can be produced in novel liaisons. Having multiple affairs allows a person to escape his or her anxieties, feel pleasure, and feel validated by being desired.

A vicious cycle of release, shame (sometimes), and desire to fend off unwanted emotions by seeking release has probably been wired into his brain — it may have become an addiction.

If his behavior is that of a sex addict, it has probably caused his self-esteem and average dopamine levels to be lowered. This will likely drive him to an even more desperate pursuit of the temporary high or relief that affairs provide.

Excitement without real courage

Novelty heightens the senses and intensifies passion. For someone who has affairs, the novelty lies in being with a new person.

Novelty with the same partner means having the courage to bring new meaning and depth to that relationship — to let oneself be known on a deeper level and to bring freshness to the relationship. To do these things, one must risk rejection.

It takes courage and a sense of adventure to go beyond the routine that inevitably establishes itself in a committed relationship, and bring the *best* of oneself to the same partner. It would be far more challenging, and ultimately rewarding, for your partner to face his fears and risk invalidation with someone who really knows him — you, *or* at least to approach you honestly in discussing the troubles in your relationship.

As for any addict, it takes a great deal of motivation and courage to learn to resist seeking the quick high that the addict has found so compelling. To rewire a neurological highway requires tremendous determination and a willingness to face emotional anxieties and resist physical cravings, and likely requires getting counseling and/or going to Sex Addicts Anonymous.

Infidelity: "Hoping and wishing my husband would give me the same love he showers on other women over ten years of infidelity."

To get a better perspective, imagine your situation in reverse. Suppose you were the unfaithful one having various affairs with other men, and that your husband put up with that kind of behavior for ten years. What would you think about your husband? Would you have any respect for him?

Excluding unusual circumstances, I think that the answer is "no."

A person has more respect for someone who shows a strong sense of self-respect. To gain self-respect, it's important to learn to set boundaries and to make decisions based on what is healthy and beneficial for the long term rather than on wishful thinking. Ultimately, you need the courage to face your fear of life without him and be prepared to act.

Unfortunately, your longing to stay with someone who does not treat you in a reciprocal loving way will not change him into someone who will love, respect, and cherish you. Staying with someone who repeatedly has affairs will only drain away any self-respect and *joie de vivre* you have left, making the situation worse.

The best way to avoid having to endure such hurtful behavior from someone is not to put up with it from the very start. Ask yourself what has kept you tied to him for so long. Is your hope that things will improve if you stay together covering up your fear of moving out on your own?

Don't be afraid to live alone. When you start choosing people and activities that enhance your life and your wellbeing, your strength and self-empowerment will grow. You will be amazed at what might turn up in your life. Let go of your fear, set some suitable boundaries, and be prepared to walk away.

"She's the codependent one!"

Fused partners who stay together for a long time, e.g., more than a year, are generally *equally* emotionally fused (codependent) although they may not think they are. They just express their codependence in different ways.

For example, it's not an accident, although it may be unconscious, that a man who seeks his own space chooses a woman who yearns for connection. If she didn't seek connection, there wouldn't be any. If he didn't seek space, there wouldn't be any. They both need the other to find some sort of balance.

Yet the man may believe that the problem is all hers — she is simply too needy. The woman believes that the problem is all his — he fears intimacy. They've both selected the ideal person either to learn from or to blame.

"I'm always walking on eggshells."

If you are walking on eggshells to avoid upsetting your partner that means you are allowing yourself to be controlled by your partner's reactivity. While it's nice to be considerate of other people's feelings, you should not do so at the expense of your own.

Differentiation

The best relationships are between people who are *differentiated*, that is, able to be emotionally objective and separate, while at the same time being intimate and caring. *Differentiation* allows you to become intensely intimate without becoming infected with another person's anxiety.

The great psychologist Murray Bowen was the first to discuss the concept of *differentiation*. "The ability to be in emotional contact with others yet still autonomous in one's emotional functioning is the essence of the concept of differentiation."[4]

Undifferentiated couples, who are emotionally *fused* or codependent, tend to fear their partner's reactions and as a result modify their behavior to avoid overreaction. Much of their conduct occurs in anticipation of their partner's desires, discomfort, or anger. They eventually may come to feel as though they have lost who they really are. Often they have.

Being true to yourself

Being true to yourself when you relate to others is what makes a relationship interesting, passionate, and sustainable. So when you feel that you have to walk on eggshells, take a moment to figure out what you actually feel and believe.

Central to differentiation is facing your discomfort with your partner's anger, cold shoulder, or other reactivity. Learn how to be diplomatic and kind to your partner, while standing firm in being true to yourself.

State calmly, "You may not like my position, but this is how I feel/what I think/what I'd like to do." When you expect a negative reaction, be prepared to accept it. If your partner becomes angry, don't take it personally. Leave the room if necessary, but with the faith that any conversation you will have will be a real conversation between two people who have enough self-respect and courage to be true to themselves and honest with the other. Only in this way can you have a truly effective conversation and a fulfilling relationship.

"He wouldn't like it if I took up something new."

Imagine ten or fifteen years of being together, when one partner decides to take up mountain climbing or to go back to school for a master's degree. Such change will result in loss — a loss of the comfort and security the couple has become used to over the years. "What if he meets someone else?" "What if she gets bored of me?"

Fearful of change, the partner may feel threatened. "What do you need to do that for? It's expensive and a waste of time," may be his or her reaction.

If you fear that your partner will feel threatened by change might cause you to avoid trying a new path. As a result of maintaining the status quo, you lose out on excitement, adventure, and growth, which means that the relationship also loses out on excitement, adventure, and growth. Possibilities and dreams are replaced by boredom, resentment, and regret.

Ironically, *lack* of change also results in loss. Predictability and stagnancy cause a loss of vitality and richness in the relationship. If there is no change, novelty and passion will be lost.

In essence, having close relationships is perilous because of the inherent risks of disappointment, loss, and heartache. Indeed, any relationship either ends or one of the partners dies. To completely avoid loss, we would have to avoid entering into any deep relationships. Thus, the willingness to tolerate loss helps us to embrace the risks and joys of love and living life fully.

If we approach love and friendship with the understanding that there will be loss of some sort, we can avoid the regrets and lost vitality that come from living in the clutches of fear. Partners may grow apart, but at least they won't stagnate together. The upside is that the relationship can develop depth and richness by means of either partner's growth.

Being needed versus being wanted: "How could he leave me? I did everything for him."

There are generally good intentions involved in being exceptionally helpful. People who "do everything" for someone usually intend to be loving and kind. Yet over-functioning often stems from an unconscious impulse to increase another person's dependence and loyalty to the relationship. The problem is that it often backfires.

Unintended consequences of cultivating dependence

All relationships involve some degree of dependence. For most people, it's quite nice when another person helps out. Yet when one person does an extravagant share of the work, the other person may start feeling engulfed and overwhelmed. He or she may feel encumbered with a growing sense of obligation to reciprocate. Obligation and desire are like oil and water. Feeling beholden toward a person causes desire for that person to fade.

When people become highly dependent on their partners, a sense of indebtedness bordering on guilt causes passion and intimacy to suffer. While it's important that partners are considerate and helpful, it's equally important to avoid letting dependency and indebtedness smother the relationship.

It feels better to be wanted than needed. Desire to be with your partner adds vitality to the relationship. Feeling obligated to reciprocate does not.

Standing back

Those who tend to over-function would improve their lives by focusing more on their own enjoyment and desires and giving their partner greater breathing room and independence. This means resisting doing everything, even at the risk that some things won't be executed as well as they would like.

As Kahlil Gibran wrote in *The Prophet*, "Love one another, but make not a bond of love: Let it rather be a moving sea between the shores of your souls."

Dysfunctional Parents: "My parents were so dysfunctional, I don't even know what a good relationship looks like."

Dancing together is a perfect metaphor for the many interactions that occur in a relationship.

Questions to consider

Ask yourself the following questions about your relationship: Do you do the dance of relationship to enjoy and connect with your partner or just to look good in front of other people? If you've ever seen the Australian comedy *Strictly Ballroom*, you can clearly see the difference between the couples with an authentic connection and those who are trying to impress the crowds with flashy smiles, choreographed moves, and peacock-feathered outfits.

Are you dancing *with* your partner or just dancing nearby, hardly ever looking at him or her? Are you critical of or embarrassed by your partner's moves? Are you more concerned with your clumsiness than with having a good time together? When one of you makes a mistake, do you move on light-heartedly, or do you punish your partner with an angry look? Or, do you berate yourself and wreck the evening with your sullenness?

The paradox of dancing together

The question at the heart of this metaphor is "How can two autonomous people desiring love and intimacy sustain their passion without becoming controlling, needy, bored, or reactive?"

The "dance" in the relationship remains most sustainable when partners dance together without being in lockstep.

Some dancers are lost without a partner who leads or follows as expected. They are incapable of being alone and independent, and as a result, they try to control the other through heavy-handedness or critical looks. Similar "symptoms" develop in a relationship. Rather than simply adapting when their partner tries something new or independently, partners who fear autonomy tend to react with anger, humiliation, or embarrassment.

On the other hand, partners who focus primarily on themselves and remain excessively separate may never make a connection at all.

When we dance together we embrace a paradox — we connect with our partner while honoring each person's individuality and letting mild missteps slide. It's the same in all relationships, not just romantic ones. We have to embrace the paradox of responding considerately to another person while honoring the music within ourselves.

Sexual Intimacy: "I've got needs, but she pretends to be asleep."

Pursuit of biological "need" is a turn-off

When you translate your desire into a need for biological gratification, it's a turn-off. Your partner will resent feeling used to feed your physical "needs" and self-esteem. Desire out of a need to be satiated is consumptive and can never be fully satisfying to either party.

Desire out of abundance

However, sexual intimacy deepens the vitality of long-term relationships and should definitely be pursued. So talk to your partner to discover how you can both deepen the intimacy between the two of you. Ask your partner what she's feeling and express how important it is for you to have passion and intimacy on all levels in your relationship.

In addition to talking to her, change your view of sexual intimacy from one of need to one of desire. Make her feel desired, loved, and cherished rather than needed.

Martin Prechtel, a Guatemalan Shaman, distinguishes between seduction — the act of getting what you want — and courting — the act of giving blessing to what you love.

This art of courting comes from desire out of abundance, which can lead to increased desire and intimacy for both partners. Desire out of fullness arises out of a sense of self worth and an appreciation for the other person.

Show her your love and appreciation. Share more of yourself. Remember those attributes that attracted you to her and tell her. Tell her your fantasies and ask her to tell you hers. You might be pleasantly surprised by the result.

"I feel so critical of my partner. I can't help pointing out every flaw."

Three negative consequences of criticism

There are three important reasons to look for the positive in your partner.

First, how you treat other people becomes who you are. Would you rather be supportive, appreciative and optimistic, or critical, stern, and mean-spirited? When you push yourself to act respectfully and overlook unimportant flaws, you will feel much better about yourself.

Second, how you judge others affects the way they behave and view themselves. When you point out how sloppy and clumsy another person is, those traits will become magnified. If instead you focus on their good qualities, those good qualities tend to intensify.

Third, constant criticism will wreck a relationship and make you both miserable.

Change yourself

If you tend to be critical, you have to purposely develop the habit of appreciating the good in others. The neuro-plasticity of our brains allows us to change, but it requires a lot of practice. Every time you think, "What a slob!" you must force yourself to think and even express a different thought about the person, such as, "He is always there for me."

After 2000 or so thought switches, it becomes almost natural to change that particular thought. It will also become easier to see the good in people around you, because people tend to thrive in an environment of appreciation. Two thousand thought switches for one negative thought may seem like a lot. However, it's amazing how many thoughts occur in one day. Even if it takes a year to make such a change, wouldn't you rather have better relationships in a year than the alternative — deterioration into misery?

Keep in mind, we are talking about moderating *excessive* criticism. There are many circumstances when it is appropriate to communicate about the other person's behavior. We should speak up about behavior that erodes the quality of the relationship, such as unhealthy habits and hygiene or excessive criticism. Unfortunately, some people are not open to criticism no matter how constructive, appropriate, and well intended.

To decide whether it is better to give constructive criticism or to resist criticizing altogether, we have to ask ourselves two things:

1.   Keeping in mind our own imperfections, how much of a particular behavior should we put up with? Obviously, if we ourselves are overly critical, which is a very annoying flaw in a relationship, we should put up with some flaws in the other person.

2.   How likely is it that constructive criticism will help the other person or enhance the relationship? If the constructive criticism is unlikely to result in change, it might be wise to put our focus on something more positive.

"I never get to go skiing anymore. My partner doesn't like to ski."

Free choice

Saying "I don't get to" implies a lack of power and control over your own life. You should not need to ask for permission. Handing over the power over your own life will only lead to resentment, which eats away at the relationship.

Passions breed passion

It's important in a relationship that both partners continue doing the things they are passionate about. If you love skiing, make sure you get out there and go skiing and encourage your partner to do what he or she loves to do. People who pursue their passions have a vitality that is irresistible and brings magic into their relationships.

185

Not doing everything together

Partners don't have to do everything together. In fact, a little space can be healthy. Tell your partner how happy it makes you to go skiing. If he or she is not interested, you can go on your own to enjoy some fresh powder, groomers, or bumps.

By feeding your soul, you become more interesting and enjoyable to be around. Even if you spend a little less time with your partner, when you're with him or her, you'll feel more alive and have something of interest to share.

"How can you be so jealous! You're being ridiculous!"

A jealous partner may have experienced abandonment when younger and as a result becomes easily triggered with feelings of jealousy. Getting angry won't help the situation. Try to have compassion. "You sound jealous. I want you to know you are the most important person to me. There is nobody else."

If jealousy continues to be an ongoing problem without any basis to it, tell the jealous person that the suspicions are hurtful and are causing you to feel defensive and that is not good for the relationship. Suggest focusing on his or her desires rather than on his or her fears in the relationship.

Try to be understanding as this is about a person's vulnerability and insecurity born out of pain. However, while you should be considerate and reassuring, don't start restricting your own life to accommodate his or her fears. This is a slippery slope that ends in a constricted and resentful relationship.

"What else should I give up to make her happy?"

My girlfriend doesn't like it when I go on bike rides with my buddies, which I like to do. She's also pressuring me to get a better job than the one I have and am happy with. How should I handle this?

Jake

Helpful or controlling?

Is her behavior helpful or controlling? She says she loves you, but you've got to get a "better" job and you shouldn't ride with your buddies. Her attempts to choose your friends, activities, and work all suggest that she considers you to be inadequate.

Your girlfriend's attempts to change you and how you spend your time may eventually undermine your free choice. Free will is an essential human drive. So when someone tries to control you, it can feel oppressive and annoying. This is why most people would rather choose their own path, even it is paved with mistakes or difficulties, than to follow someone else's direction.

To sustain a fulfilling relationship based on connection *and* autonomy, you must draw a critical boundary between receiving suggestions and following direction.

Trying to improve

People who spend a lot of time managing people around them may simply want to make others happy or have things done "right" — right in their view. Yet controlling people often experience discomfort with another person's independence. They may be too busy directing others to notice what's going on within themselves. If they were to notice, they may find that they have difficulty regulating their own anxiety.

Control undermines respect

Even when the controlling partner wants the best for the other person, too much management by one partner will damage the mutual respect necessary for a truly loving relationship. Doing everything together, having the same friends, and agreeing all the time only creates the illusion of intimacy. In time, the relationship is likely to lose passion and ultimately become dull or oppressive.

Appreciate the unexpected

Relationships that are fresh and alive require that the two individuals are each in control of their own lives. To experience passion, you need to be able to handle and appreciate the unexpected in life, similar to the way a good traveler enjoys unforeseen events as adventure. Part of the allure and mystery in a relationship comes from allowing your partner to choose his or her own path, passions, friends, and work.

People who tend to control other people often experience negative tension when there is uncertainty. Anything unpredictable causes considerable anxiety. Since there is so much in life over which we have no control, it's important to learn to live with the discomfort of not always being in control.

Those who are controlling

Those who are tempted to control others need to stand back, relax, and let live. Rather than telling others what to do, you might recount your own experiences. You can give your opinion, but do so without manipulation. State how you feel and why, but without badgering, whining, demanding, or maneuvering.

Controlling people need to learn to accept their own anxiety when they allow others to make their own decisions. There's actually some relief when you let go of the tension that accompanies constant management of other people.

Those who are easily controlled

The person who complains about a controlling partner is also an active participant in the dance of control. Generally, those who are susceptible to being controlled are trying to avoid confrontation. The problem with living in dread of your partner's reactions is that your desires and values wither away, which leads to a restricted, lackluster life and a passionless relationship.

Those who are susceptible to being controlled need to stop fearing the other person's reactions. That doesn't mean becoming confrontational. You simply cannot let the fear of another person's anger dictate your willingness to stand up for your values and needs. Candid, honest communication is best.

Passion

Passion is the feeling of exhilaration in the face of mystery. It doesn't exist in the context of restriction and uniformity. Passion arises from the heat generated by the intermingling of two people pursuing their own individual goals. So if partners sacrifice their personal interests, opinions, and friends for the sake of their relationship, that relationship will probably lose its passion.

Get a better job?

So to answer your question, Jake, rather than arguing or giving in to your girlfriend, you will both benefit from an open and honest discussion about what your needs and desires are regarding your work.

You can also gain a lot of insight into her expectations by asking her *why* she wants you to get a "better" job. If her expectations don't match yours, you will avoid a lot of heartache and disappointment by being clear about your own aspirations early on. The following questions can illuminate what is beneath her prodding you about your work.

- Does she hope that you would be happier with a different job?
- Does she want to improve your status or image?
- Does she want you to make more money?
- Or does she have faith in your ability to do something you don't have faith in yourself to do?

This may be a good opportunity to discuss key values you each have. Clarify how your values may differ from hers. For instance, if she thinks you will be happier with the other job because you'll make more money, clarify what you value about your current job, whether it's the actual work, the free time, or the people you work with, for example.

Stop biking with your friends?

First consider whether you spend enough quality time together. Perhaps you are not putting in enough effort toward the relationship. Or perhaps the two of you have different expectations regarding relationships. This is the time to find out.

Under pressure to stay home rather than to ride with your buddies, you might say, "It means a lot to me to spend time and ride with my buddies."

It's worth exploring what your girlfriend's fears are and to address them.

- Does she feel insecure about the relationship? She may think that loving couples spend all their time together.
- Perhaps you value autonomy more than she does.
- Or perhaps she feels that you are focusing on fun at the expense of your responsibilities.
- Or she might think that you have lost interest in her.

These issues are important to discuss early in the relationship. Without clarifying your values with candor, you might end up living in constant dread of your girlfriend's reactivity.

Healthy compromise rather than control

Avoiding control and manipulation doesn't mean there shouldn't be any compromise. Healthy compromise involves respecting free choice and valuing both persons' needs. When people agree to compromise without having been manipulated, they are often willing to accommodate their partners' real needs *without* resenting them afterwards. Instead of being motivated by fear of the partner's reactions, each partner strives for maximum happiness for *both* partners. Yet each allows the other to have the ultimate say in choosing his or her own path to a happy and meaningful life.

Blamed for being Attractive:
"My husband accuses me of being flirtatious, which I'm not. People are just drawn to me."

There's a big difference between provocatively flirting with others and simply being an outgoing, attractive person. People with self-respect who are engaged in the world with a positive outlook tend to have a certain magnetism that is appealing to others.

It is very likely that it is those alluring qualities that attracted your husband to you in the first place. You must not let him try to change the way you are because he fears that others will be attracted to those same qualities.

A vibrant person exudes a healthy vitality that should not be misconstrued as an act of betrayal. People cannot expect their partners to go out in the world with a stern or repressed demeanor and then come home feeling radiant and happy.

By accusing you of being flirtatious, he is unconsciously trying to shame you into hiding the part of yourself that is animated and engaging. Keep in mind he may be doing this because he fears losing you. The unfortunate result is that he will push you away and cause you to hide the more vibrant part of yourself from *him*.

Thus, it's vital that he show his appreciation for the part of you that captivates people. You might remind him that *he's* the one you are faithful to (assuming it's true, of course), and that he should not expect you to constrict yourself around others in your sphere. Remind him that you are *not* interested in starting up inappropriate relationships and that you know your boundaries.

Ask him not to diminish himself by blaming you for your charismatic life force. Instead, if he learns to overcome his insecurity, he'll be more attractive by exuding more confidence in himself. By valuing what attracted him to you in the first place, rather than trying to squelch your spark, he would enhance the magic between you.

"Why are you looking at her? You think she's more attractive than me, don't you?"

Neediness

Many relationship problems have two primary causes:
1. Fear of losing the other person, and
2. Attempts to avoid anxiety.

When the fear of losing the other person combines with attempts to avoid anxiety, a person may take on the ineffective attitude of neediness, and even desperation. Often when we're anxious, we seek comfort and validation from others. Others may then feel obliged to provide us with ongoing validation because they feel uncomfortable with our anxiety.

- *Yes, you're more attractive than she is.*
- *Yes, I love you.*
- *No, I don't wish I were with someone more talented, thinner, and smarter.*

The more you feel pressured to validate another person, the sooner desire and passion will be replaced by obligation and dread.

Validation coerced through neediness differs from authentic appreciation. The latter is freely-given, not an attempt to mitigate distress.

Diminishing boundaries

Emotional fusion breaks down boundaries and causes increasingly infectious anxiety.

The underlying problem is that wellbeing cannot be provided by another person without diminishing the other person's sense of independence and self-empowerment. When there are too many strings attached to the approval or help you are receiving, important boundaries to your sense of self become blurred. It will no longer feel very good to be emotionally or financially "taken care of" by the other person, whether it's your partner, friend, or parent, when the corresponding sense of indebtedness intensifies. The expectation that you *have to* reciprocate and provide for the other person's wellbeing increases pressure, anxiety, and disappointment in both partners.

"I can't stand it when my partner seems to be attracted to someone else."

Most friendships are based on some sort of attraction, in that we are drawn to various qualities of our friends.

Jealousy

Unless you are the jealous type who is constantly jealous, jealousy is usually a signal alerting you to pay attention to what's going on in your relationship. It serves as a warning, but should not be used as a reason to become antagonistic and possessive. Often jealousy is a product of projecting your own history on to another person. Yet it may be a wakeup call to put more effort into the relationship or to explore why it is that your partner is attracted to a particular person. Of course, it could also indicate that there is something more serious going on, in which case you may need to take action to protect yourself emotionally and/or financially.

No relationship has it all

Attraction to another person may indicate what is missing in your life and/or your primary relationship. No relationship can fulfill every aspect of your desires, because every relationship is limited by the experiences and capacities of the two people involved. Nor can you expect to satisfy your partner's every need and wish — e.g., to enjoy the same sports, parent with the same style, have the same spending habits, have the same spiritual aspirations, like the same friends, have the same sexual desire at the same time, etc.

Using attraction to indicate what could improve

Attractions point out the qualities we are ready to bring into our lives. For example, a couple might have a financially stable situation, a secure family life, and an active social life. Yet there might be a lot of potential for growth in the area of sensuality, adventure, or spirituality. The husband may find himself repeatedly drawn to sensuous women, or the wife might be drawn to rugged adventurers.

In contrast, someone whose partner is spontaneous but a bit unpredictable and irresponsible might be drawn to grounded, stable types.

When you realize that there is something missing or one-sided in your relationship, as there is in every relationship, there's an opportunity to grow in that direction. For example, the practical type could make efforts to become more sensual; the predictable type might ask his or her partner to take an adventurous trip; the unpredictable type might work on staying within the budget and following through on promises.

Learning from the attraction

Ask yourself what it is that draws your partner to the other person. For example, is it her ability to listen to him without criticizing him? Is it his carefree attitude? Is it her freedom from household and family concerns? Is it his interest in intellectual matters? Is it her warmth and openness to others? Or his ability to contain his emotions and listen rather than talk?

The objective is not to become like the man or woman your partner is attracted to currently. The point is to become aware of the way in which your relationship may have become one-sided. If you are perceptive, you may find an opportunity for you to grow and your relationship to improve.

Avoiding destructive affairs

The sooner we consider what specific attractions mean for our partners and ourselves, the less likely they will turn into destructive affairs. Cultivating qualities that have been dormant or absent enhances our own life and relationships. Moreover, by cultivating lost or missing qualities in our own authentic way will often cause the outside attraction to subside.

Examples:

- A man wonders why his wife is drawn to a self-indulgent man. He realizes that frugality has been pervasive in their marriage and has led to financial security, but is now unnecessarily constricting their marriage. If they loosen up the purse strings just a bit and enjoy some of the fruits of their work together, the outside attraction may diminish over time and the couple's new enjoyment will add another dimension to their relationship.

- The opposite could hold true in a relationship involving an overly-indulgent, impulsive partner. A person accustomed to a partner who splurges recklessly might become drawn to somebody with foresight and self-restraint to provide the grounding and security lacking in the primary relationship.

- If the other man seems to be a Bohemian artist type, ask yourself if your life together has become too conventional. This could be an opportunity to allow your creativity to seek expression.

- If the other woman seems to be truly interested in what your husband says, you may realize that over the years you have paid less attention to what he says. No one likes to be treated as though he or she isn't worthy of attention, especially in an intimate relationship. It may be time to refocus.

- If the other woman is very alluring, perhaps this is an area that has been ignored amidst the practicalities of family life. It may be time to find ways to develop your more sensuous, romantic, fun, and sexy side.

Desire begins within each of us and is not the responsibility of the other person. You might ask yourself how could you feel more desirable again and allow that part of yourself to smolder once more.

Gradual change

It is quite exciting, particularly later in life, to discover your inner athlete when you've been in the office most of the time, or to discover your inner Aphrodite when you've been tending to the home and children. If we are more open about what attracts us and what we desire in our lives, we can help each other to develop a more multifaceted intimacy than we had ever dared imagine.

However, when we develop new parts of ourselves, we want to make sure that we don't devalue the primary parts of ourselves, which have significant value. Real integration of new qualities only occurs when we do not cast aside the primary parts of our personality. Thus, transformation can occur organically and often within the existing relationship, without the dramatic swings that are painful to everyone involved.

"I think my husband is having an emotional affair with another woman. Since it's not sexual, it doesn't matter."

Friendships

Healthy friendships and attractions do not need to threaten a marriage or long-term committed relationship. In fact they often add richness and enjoyment to life. Yet the fact that this relationship feels like an emotional "affair" suggests that it is supplanting the emotional bond between the two of you. When an attraction turns into an affair or an obsession, physical or emotional, it can hurt everyone involved. The intensity or secrecy of such a relationship can result in a sense of betrayal that is insidious to the primary relationship.

Emotional vs. sexual affair

The question as to whether an emotional or sexual affair is worse varies from person to person. A sexual affair, except in unusual circumstances, is a betrayal of the intimacy of the primary relationship. An emotional affair can be just as painful if the intimacy and time spent together is inordinate and thus damages the primary relationship.

How to respond in a self-empowered way

Your power is reflected in how you respond to your partner's relationship to the other person. Avoid becoming embittered or defensive, both of which are unattractive and weak positions. Rather than impulsively ending the relationship or blaming yourself, first ask how your relationship could improve.

The answer may require that you take an honest look at how you have each participated in the situation. Very often in long-term relationships, couples become preoccupied with work, raising children, and the practicalities of a household or social life, and let the adventure, fun, and romance in the relationship dwindle. Also consider whether you have started taking your partner for granted or become overly critical or blasé about the relationship. An outside attraction can be a wakeup call that you may need to re-ignite your own inner spark.

Speaking to your partner

It can be surprisingly helpful to communicate openly about such matters despite taboos against doing so, but only if you can do so from a position of emotional strength and honest vulnerability, without attacking, falling apart, or pleading.

Your demeanor is more important than your choice of words. Although you may feel vulnerable, it is more effective and attractive to contain yourself when having such a salient conversation. You need to balance candid vulnerability with self-empowerment. Speaking from a position of strength without being cold engenders the respect you seek.

Look at the two following scenarios and imagine how effective either would be in strengthening your primary relationship.

1. Crying and angry, desperate and fearful: "Why do you spend so much time with her? Don't you love me anymore?"

2. Speaking with compassion and personal empowerment as well as concern and sadness: "I love you and want to stay with you, but I only want to stay with you if we are both fully committed to having the best relationship with each other we can."

Depending on the situation, you might ask your husband to spend less time with the other person. You may suggest to him that you do some specific and enjoyable things together. Also make sure that you pursue some of your own passions and activities that you have been neglecting.

If the time or energy your partner spends with the other person becomes excessive, you may decide to ask your partner to stop spending time with the person in question and you may put forth an ultimatum. You are more likely to be successful if you speak from a place of empowerment and understanding rather than from anger or desperation. You may have to use a lot of willpower to remain calm. Remember that by doing so, you will maintain more self-respect and have the best chance of improving relations or moving on if you have to.

If he seems uninterested in making an effort, make sure you still go out and pursue your interests and see your friends – you will be far more desirable and you will be less likely to become depressed. If your partner continues to ignore your requests, then you may benefit from seeing a couples' therapist. Ultimately, if you decide to terminate the relationship, it's best to do so from with some understanding rather than with hostility.

"I want us to be closer and I'd like more approval."

What counts in making a happy marriage is not so much how compatible you are, but how you deal with incompatibility.

~George Levinger

Most people and even some therapists confuse intimacy with closeness. They think relationships will improve if people communicate with more approval and accommodation. Intimacy and passion, however, do not thrive where there is complete agreement and approval between two people.

Beware of Fusion

In fact, too much agreement and feigned empathy can result in fusion, which does not enhance intimacy, but destroys it. Fusion is the dissolution of boundaries between people, which causes anxiety to become extremely infectious.[5] Intimacy, on the other hand, requires that people are emotionally separate, and thus do not overreact to their partner's anxiety. Note that overreaction includes feigning agreement to keep the peace.

Manipulation

Fusion often arises when partners pressure each other through manipulation or complaints to give validation and approval.

- "Don't you love me?"

- "Don't you agree with me?"
- "Don't you think what she said to me is terrible!"
- "I can't believe you could think that!"

There is nothing wrong with enjoying approval from others. It's only when we pressure others to give us approval that we dampen the spark in the relationship. Coercion and a sense of obligation to boost your partner's self-esteem destroy the vitality of a relationship. Acquiescence replaces authenticity.

Dependence

Another problem with fusion is that you become dependent on another person's approval. As David Schnarch points out, to hand over your sense of self as well as your security is tantamount to saying "Here's my sense of self-worth — take care of it, or else I won't take care of yours."[6] Codependence based on fear will run the show, rather than autonomous choice and affection.

Concealing yourself

When we become dependent on the approval of others, we start concealing parts of ourselves that may not get the desired approval. Instead we only show those aspects that generate approval. We accommodate our partner's point of view rather than challenge ourselves and our partners with fresh thinking and honesty.

Examples of self-concealment

- "I'd better laugh at her joke or she'll be hurt."
- "I'd better not leave her side at this party, or she'll feel insecure."
- "I'd better not wear this stunning dress, or he'll be upset if other men see me looking beautiful."
- "I'd better not talk about quantum mechanics, or he'll feel inadequate."

While it may be wise or kind to tell a white lie occasionally, *regularly* screening your true opinions to accommodate another person is antithetical to intimacy. When you hide parts of yourself and stop growing, you limit yourself, rather than become a more whole and multifaceted individual. As more and more aspects of yourself remain unexpressed, fear of rejection increases. When you stifle yourself, you stagnate. You shrivel up and eventually resent your partner for robbing you of your vitality.

Controlling behavior

If your sense of identity or wellbeing depends on what your partner thinks and does, it's natural to want to control your partner. So you attempt to get your partner to do things and think in a way that you believe will eliminate anxiety and promote his or her validation of you. In order to deal with your own anxiety you try to pacify your partner.

The problem is that control stifles spontaneity, freshness, and passion in a relationship. You hesitate to do new things or have a differing opinion out of fear of your partner's disapproval. For example, people who complain of sexual boredom are often unaware that they themselves feel threatened by the display of new sexual behavior by their partner. Moreover, through ridicule or rejection they may embarrass their partner to avoid revealing their own insecurity in such matters.[7]

Differentiation and intimacy

People who are differentiated take responsibility for their own emotions. They don't live their lives as a reaction to their fear of intimacy or their fear of solitude. As a result, they can be intimate without becoming controlling and pressuring others to validate them.

By not allowing other people's anxiety to infect them, differentiated people remain emotionally separate and objective, which paradoxically allows for greater connection and deeper intimacy. Relationships are desired and appreciated with gratitude, rather than controlled to fulfill a need.

"I can't stand it when he disagrees with me."

Emotional fusion

Do you feel threatened when your partner doesn't agree with you or behave the way you want?

If so, you may be seeking a type of unity that is both unattainable and undesirable. When people in a relationship feel alienated from one another, *emotional fusion* is more often the problem than insufficient attachment.[8] *Emotional fusion* occurs when people do not function independently. Instead they are emotionally reactive to each other by being overly acquiescent or rebellious, or oscillating between the two.

Forms of manipulation

Couples use silence, withdrawal, and facial expressions of disapproval to pressure each other to agree or give approval. These forms of manipulation, used with varying degrees of subtlety, usually cause people to become defensive or to repress feelings and thoughts that are incompatible with those of their partner.

Where's the passion?

If partners cannot handle differences of opinion, they miss the opportunity to have energized discussions between two individuals expressing their own thoughts. Eventually passion in the relationship will disappear because it can only persist between two *separate* individuals. Passion requires heat. While it may seem nice to be in agreement, too much conformity usually causes mystery, growth, and passion to fade away and be replaced by predictability, boredom, and/or anger and resentment.

Acquiescence leads to repression

The partner who is pressured to agree often will accommodate his or her partner, while repressing conflicting feelings and thoughts. Over time the couple no longer has much to talk about because both partners hesitate to share incompatible or new parts of themselves. This ongoing avoidance of sharing critical parts of themselves results in partners drifting apart because they cannot truly know each other. You have to express your vulnerabilities in order to truly be seen and known.

Repressed parts of the personality then gather energy in the unconscious, and ultimately seep out in the form of depression, resentment, sickness, outbursts, or secret affairs. Repressed feelings and thoughts often erupt unexpectedly in anger, violence, and even unexpected divorce. How often have we heard the question, "I did everything for him, how could he leave me?"

Repression leads to anger

When someone cannot tolerate another person's disagreement or disapproval, he or she often becomes controlling, angry, and sometimes violent. When the other person wants to disagree but fears the controlling party's anger, objectionable thoughts and opinions get repressed, while resentment grows.

Arguing and conflict in a relationship are often manifestations of the unconscious attempting to balance two basic human drives — to obtain emotional contact and to retain autonomy. Arguing provides *emotional contact*, while anger and resistance to one's partner's wishes promote *autonomy*.

Honesty

When you are emotionally separate from another person, you don't need to become angry to create separation. You don't need dramatic expressions of self-assertion to resist pressure to merge or agree with another person. You can be honest without being hostile. You can express disagreement without being angry or scared. Uncomfortable, yes; angry, no.

"I'm not going to visit my brother because my wife will get mad."

Fear of being alone

Underlying most controlling behavior is a fear of being left alone, physically or emotionally. A person's reactivity and possessiveness is often driven by anxiety and fear of abandonment.

The problem is that we can never be fully united in thought and feeling with another person. In fact, the more we try to possess another person or allow ourselves to be controlled, the more we squeeze the magic out of the relationship.

Once we genuinely accept our existential separation from others, we can enjoy the connection we have more fully, however fleeting it may be. Then we can be truly loving without becoming controlling and possessive.

Responding to a controlling person

If you are in a relationship with a controlling partner who is trying to coerce you into not doing something reasonable that you want to do, such as visiting your brother, you can choose to respond in the following ways:

1. **Accommodate** — You don't go visit your brother, but you will feel disappointed, angry, disempowered, and resentful for not going.

2. **Rebel** — You vehemently declare that you're going anyway, but your partner will try to punish you with his anger.

3. **Differentiate** — You are considerate while maintaining your self-respect. You tell her you'll miss her and you're sorry she'll be lonely, but it's really important for you to spend some time with your brother. Or, you could say that you'd really like to see your brother, but that she is welcome to join you if she can get away. If your partner continues to be angry about your decision, you can show compassion to a point, but you should not allow yourself to be manipulated by another person's fear or anger. Stand firm albeit with compassion, but without becoming defensive.

Intimacy requires freedom

It sounds paradoxical that intimacy and passion can deepen as we accept our separateness and stop controlling others or allowing ourselves to be controlled. Yet a relationship based on respect requires letting go of fear and control. By breaking away from control and possessiveness, we can allow a little unpredictability and excitement back into the relationship.

Passion is based on the feeling of being alive, alert and excited in the midst of the unknown. By respecting another person's autonomy and embracing the associated anxiety, we can enhance excitement, desire, and passion in our relationship with that person.

As we face and accept our own existential separateness, our tolerance for being alone increases. In addition, our disappointment in others diminishes, because we relinquish unrealistic expectations that our partners will save us from ourselves.

"I can't live with her and I can't live without her."

When someone drives you crazy, yet you can't stand the idea of being apart, you are probably too emotionally fused with that person. This is also known as being codependent. Emotional fusion creates two paradoxical feelings — a need for more emotional contact and a desire to get away. An emotionally-fused relationship becomes infused with contrary feelings of being trapped and controlled, and being isolated and unsupported.

The problem is that neither partner can maintain his or her sense of identity and groundedness in the presence of the other.

Both people take everything personally and become reactive by withdrawing coldly or picking a fight. They swing between attack and capitulation. Bitterness and frustration cause the couple to withdraw from each other, but when apart, they feel unbalanced and empty. Any connection at this point, even bitter fighting, makes them feel more alive than when alone.

Differentiation[9]

To resolve the anguish of emotional fusion, individuals need to become more highly *differentiated*, that is, emotionally separate, and therefore, less reactive.

Differentiation will

1.   permit you to get intensely involved with another person — emotionally, intellectually, physically — without becoming infected with the other person's anxiety, and

2.   eliminate the need to withdraw from or control the other person to modulate your own emotional wellbeing.

Ironically, becoming more emotionally objective and separate allows you to become more intimate. Although you may think that falling apart with anxiety shows that you care, it is actually a self-centered and ineffective way to respond to your own anxiety. It causes people to focus more on *you* instead of the problem at hand.

Someone who is differentiated may care just as deeply or more so about a person or a difficult situation but is able to contain his or her emotions. This allows a person to bring rationality and wisdom to a situation rather than simply add to the anxiety that is spiraling out of control.

Even if only one person becomes less reactive, the situation will improve.

While you want to be considerate of those close to you, you do not want to be excessively worried about their reactions. True intimacy means you can express yourself, your thoughts, and your emotions freely and deeply without emotional manipulation. When you retain some objectivity and stay calm in the face of another person's anxiety, you can grow emotionally and intellectually, often enticing the other person to do the same.

"I don't want to upset my husband by my going back to school."

Sadly education can threaten a marriage when one partner's sense of security in the relationship depends on his or her feeling superior.

The risk that one person surpasses the other in a particular area of expertise is real. Yet the answer is not to stay in a comfort zone that we imagine will secure the relationship because that is likely to lead to a stifled and passionless relationship. Keeping yourself from pursuing growth and education so as to appease your partner's insecurity will only lead to your own resentment and a stagnant relationship.

The solution is to continue to grow, while telling your partner that you love him and that you hope that he will be happy for you because it makes you happy. Hopefully, he will feel inspired to pursue his own interests and become more multifaceted as well.

You can remind him that the heart of a relationship lies in that intangible interaction of energy, where meaning comes from the magic and love between two people more than from their education and skill level.

Comparing ourselves

Our tendency to judge and compare ourselves to others stems from the emphasis our culture places on competition and "success." While competition often motivates and inspires us, it can also thwart our desire to develop in our own unique way. Unfortunately, comparisons can sometimes create feelings of inferiority or superiority that negatively affect our interaction with others.

If you feel superior to your partner because of your education, your condescending attitude prevents mutually loving interaction. If you suffer from feelings of inferiority, your feelings of being less-than also dampen the connection between you and your partner.

Uniqueness

When you put too much emphasis on how you compare to others, especially your partner, you forget to develop qualities that cannot be measured. When you stand apart to rank, categorize and pigeonhole yourself and others, you lose sight of the essence of who you are. Only when you appreciate your life without comparing yourself to other people — when you are comfortable in your own skin — can you truly link with another person.

The benefit of encouraging your partner

There are great benefits in encouraging a partner to pursue his or her own path, whether it involves further education or pursuit of other interests. First of all, there is nothing more loving and irresistibly attractive than having someone support you and believe in your endeavors and efforts. It builds your confidence when you take on challenges. It also promotes a reciprocal desire to encourage your partner to find his or her own way of self-fulfillment, thus enriching both lives. Recall how Jack Nicholson's character in the film *As Good as it Gets* won over Helen Hunt's character by his heart-felt compliment, "You make me want to be a better man."

Happiness is contagious

British researcher Nick Powdthavee found that "a married man is significantly more satisfied with his life when his wife becomes more satisfied with hers, and vice versa."[10] In fact, his research showed that happiness can overflow from one spouse to the other. Happiness is contagious even for a partner facing difficulties. Interestingly, the same results were not seen among unmarried couples who lived together.

So if further education makes you or your spouse happy, you should both be happy for the increased happiness level of the marriage.

Education empowers

Education empowers people by engendering your thinking with more nuance and complexity, an ability that can be transferred to different areas. Like any power, it can be used for good or for harm, to dominate people who know less or to empower people and enrich life.

Appreciation, not embarrassment

Being with someone who has more knowledge in a certain area is like playing tennis with someone who plays a better game. He or she can either demolish you on the court or help you play a better game yourself. Similarly, the expert tennis player will enjoy the game more when the weaker player does not feel embarrassed and awkward, but appreciates the challenge and pleasure of playing against a talented partner.

Therefore, it's best to enjoy the ways in which your partner excels and support his or her growth, while you pursue your own interests with equal gratitude. The more you embrace the capacities and unique paths of friends and loved ones, the more your own world becomes infused with the fullness of their lives.

---

[1] Recommended: Hal and Sidra Stone's *Partnering: A New Kind of Relationship.*

[2] Gottman, J. *Why Marriages Succeed or Fail.*

[3] Recommended: David Schnarch's *Passionate Marriage.*

[4] Kerr, M. & Bowen, M. *Family Evaluation.* p. 145.

[5] Kerr, M. & Bowen, M. *Family Evaluation.*

[6] Schnarch, D. *Passionate Marriage*

[7] Schnarch, D. *Constructing the Sexual Crucible.*

[8] Kerr, M. & Bowen, M. *Family Evaluation.*

[9] Murray Bowen developed the notion of *differentiation.*

[10] Powdthavee, N. *The Happiness Equation: The Surprising Economics of Our Most Valuable Asset.*

7. Thinking and the Brain

Text... phone call... email...
"Oh...what were you saying?"

What happens to your memory when you multi-task? Will texting and cell phone interruptions mingled into your face-to-face conversations weaken your effectiveness and destroy intimacy?

Research shows that a person who is interrupted takes 50% longer to complete a given task and will make 50% more mistakes.[1] Fragmented attention does not allow you to focus on any one undertaking long enough to code it into your memory well. Poor memory leads to the frustration of making mistakes and wasting time.

Perhaps more importantly, fragmented attention does not make the person you're talking with feel valued. When you are distracted by your phone and can't follow what the other person is saying, it appears that you don't care very much about that person. When somebody matters to you, you tend to pay attention.

Focused attention

Focused attention is essential to "working memory," which is equivalent to what used to be called "short-term memory." Neuropsychologist John Arden explains that, "if working memory is impaired, long-term memory will experience a famine of new information. If the road to long-term memory through working memory is blocked, the 'supplies' (memories) can't get through."[2]

If, for example, you are texting during dinner while conversing with your family, your focus will be fragmented and your working memory jeopardized. When you are distracted, you forget the detail of the story being told — your working memory hasn't been encoded into your prefrontal cortex yet. You might have caught a word or two but not the full meaning. So you have to ask, "What were you just saying?" after glancing at your text.

How to cultivate your memory

Paying attention is key to good memory. Arden recommends the following to cultivate your memory:

1.   Resist having your attention fragmented. Put the distractions aside.

2.   Schedule text messaging, phone calls, and facebooking to specific times of the day when others don't want your attention.

3.   Focus your attention on each task until it is completed. With better prefrontal cortex activation, your working memory will function well enough to code information into your long-term memory.

When you cultivate your memory, you will have a better chance to be present for the work at hand and the people in your life.

"I remember exactly what happened. These are the facts!"

Sixty Minutes recently did a story on people with "superior autobiographical memory" — those who can remember almost every day of their lives, such as what they had for lunch on April 7th, 1992.[3] Each memory is as vivid as if the event occurred yesterday. For people with such an extraordinary memory, "the past is never dead, it is not even past" — as William Faulkner once said.

Avoiding remorse

What struck me most was one woman's comment that her uncanny memory motivated her to live every day of her life in such a way that she could live with her all-too-vivid memories — memories presumably about the way she treated people and the choices she made. The fact that very little would be forgotten meant that she wanted to minimize regrets and remorse, which would always stay with her.

We can all benefit from living every day so as to mitigate regret and remorse. Even without a good memory all of us can benefit from being compassionate toward others despite their mistakes and weaknesses. That compassion must also extend toward ourselves for our own mistakes and flaws.

Arguing over the facts

Leslie Stahl, an anchor for the acclaimed 60 Minutes, asked these highly gifted people whether others found it hard to have relationships with them, as no one could ever win an argument about facts with them. They didn't think so. Knowing that they had superior memories, others stopped arguing over facts with them all together.

This may be a good lesson for everyone — to stop arguing over facts. Generally, incessant arguments over facts are not about facts at all. Instead, they are about underlying irritations or hard feelings. If we stop arguing about the facts, we have a chance to look at what is really bothering us.

Directing our focus

How about the rest of us? Many of us can't remember much more than the highlights and the low points of our lives. Is it a blessing to be able to forget?

It depends. As Joyce Appleby put it, "Our sense of worth, of wellbeing, even our sanity depends upon our remembering. But, alas, our sense of worth, our wellbeing, our sanity also depend upon our forgetting."

Rather than clinging to our memories or trying to forget, we can improve life and relationships by directing our focus. By learning from our past experiences, we can concentrate on the positive within ourselves and others. Whether we remember every detail of our lives or only the drama, it's up to us to decide what to focus on as we move forward.

"It's just the way I am. I have a bad temper and can't change it."

According to neuropsychological research, people *can* change their personality traits. However, it takes a great deal of determination and self-discipline to do so. For example, if you tend to lose your temper easily when frustrated, it takes a lot of effort to learn to stay calm. But it can be done.

Ingraining new behavior

Each time you succeed in repeating your new desired behavior, such as staying calm, generating a good mood, or not taking a drink when you feel like it, it becomes just a bit easier to transition into the desired behavior the next time.

The neuro-plasticity of the brain allows new neural connections to be formed throughout your life. Every time you repeat a new behavior, the networks in the orbitofrontal cortex become a little more efficient at re-enforcing that behavior — the neural pathways run more quickly, like a road that's being cleared of obstacles and then paved.

With each repetition, PET scan studies show that the associated brain regions work progressively more rapidly and skillfully. Axons branch out and new synapses form, creating greater efficiency and ease for the next attempt to resist the old behavior and employ the new one.

Thus, purposely letting loose your anger to "free yourself" of the emotion is not effective. While it *is* important for a person to recognize anger, look at what's causing it, and sometimes to express it, it is rarely effective to express anger by venting, raging and exploding. Such expressions usually have the opposite effect from what is intended. Rather than diminishing the anger, angry outbursts of temper help ingrain outbursts into your brain.

Willpower and repetition

So there is some truth to the adage that it takes willpower to change a bad habit. The less frequently you lose your temper, the weaker the neural connections encoded for that behavior become, and the less prone you are to lose your temper in the future. Yet if anger remains repressed, it also risks eruption. Thus it is important to replace a hot temper with self-awareness and effective communication.

The important thing is to repeat the desired habit. Soon it will become ingrained and quite natural — a new way of being.

> *We cannot solve our problems with the same thinking we used when we created them.*
>
> ~Albert Einstein

"I'm just going to make a snap decision."

We all make mistakes. Often. The best we can do to avoid making big mistakes is to avoid making big decisions *impulsively*. Significant decisions made in haste without consideration are the ones that are most often regretted.

Impulsive actions

Impulsive decisions are generated from just one part of ourselves, usually the part that's been held back for a while.

For example, after years of being the responsible type, a person might crave fun and spontaneity. This new desire may lead a person to quit a job, leave a marriage, or move to Hawaii to surf.

While any of these might be a good decision for a particular individual, making the snap decision to swing to the opposite lifestyle often leads to deep regret. Such decisions tend to backfire and cause the person to get right back on the previous track without integrating any of the new qualities a person may be seeking — in this case, spontaneity

Gradual Integration

Good decisions are the product of consideration of many factors. Generally, big life changes are most successful if they don't involve a change to the polar opposite. Instead, new qualities should be gradually integrated into your life without throwing out the qualities you've spent your life developing.

On the other hand, it's important to remember that *avoiding* making important decisions *is* a decision in itself. Life is a series of choices, experiences, and adjustments. While we shouldn't be paralyzed by the fear of making a mistake, the complete absence of decisions and adjustments can just as easily lead to big mistakes.

"I've carefully examined the pros and cons, and think I should buy this home."

Which of the following do you think is the best strategy for making significant decisions?

1. Make an immediate decision,
2. Take some time to think about the pros and cons and then decide, or
3. Consider the pros and cons, then forget about it and do something else, and later come back to make a decision?

It turns out that people are happiest with their decisions when they do #3, that is, take time out after thorough analysis, get distracted from thinking about the issue, which allows the subconscious to mull it over, and then make a decision based on reason *and* intuition.[4]

The unconscious can help

The unconscious gets blamed for a lot of emotional upheaval. Yet when decisions are complex, the unconscious is able to contribute vital information inaccessible to the conscious mind.

Conscious thought focuses well on straightforward issues. Conscious decision-making processes, such as listing pros and cons and studying statistics, are best used when there are just a few concrete variables in the decision, as in the decision of what washing machine to buy.

The unconscious, on the other hand, has a holistic ability to do parallel processing and access countless hidden clues about you, the people around you, and the situations that the conscious mind does not access easily. It can pick up obscure patterns and connections, as well as hidden emotional and physical cues.

Accessing the unconscious

The unconscious works best on a particular problem when the conscious, rational mind is distracted by some other endeavor, and therefore, cannot interfere with the unconscious.

"I better sleep on it" is a wonderful way to allow the unconscious to uncover those key factors in making a big decision such as deciding whether to buy a particular home or jump into a particular venture with a friend. If you're thinking of buying a home, the unconscious has access to subtle cues like smells, views, the emotional impact, the feeling of the neighborhood, and perhaps clues about construction quality not picked up consciously.

In this age of rapid communication, people can make better decisions when they resist the temptation to make snap decisions or to only list the pros and cons. After using objective reasoning, they might take a bike ride, sleep on it, watch a movie, or take a couple of weeks before making big, final decisions and see what the unconscious has to contribute.

> *It is no good getting furious if you get stuck. What I do is keep thinking about the problem but work on something else. Sometimes it is years before I see the way forward. In the case of information loss and black holes, it was 29 years.*
>
> ~Stephen Hawking

Fears and Phobias: "I avoid going out in public because I don't like talking to strangers."

Avoidance

When you fear certain situations, your natural tendency is to avoid them. If you feel uncomfortable at parties or talking to strangers, you tend to avoid putting yourself in situations that will arouse the related anxiety. Avoidance *seems* to be effective because in the short term your fear decreases. You feel safer staying at home.

However, brain research shows that avoidance actually causes your fear to grow over the long term.[5] Paradoxically, avoiding what you fear amplifies your anxiety. Simply thinking about situations you fear intensifies your fear and panic when the actual situation arises.

Gradual exposure

Therapy can often help by carefully exposing the fearful person to the very situations that create the initial anxiety. Repeated exposure to the source of a person's anxiety will cause the hypersensitivity to weaken.

Exposure should *not* be extreme, especially in the beginning. Otherwise, the fear intensifies too much. So if you don't like crowds, don't go from the privacy of your living room to Times Square or Yankee Stadium on the Fourth of July.

If people who are fearful of talking to strangers were to approach a person to ask for the time or directions, or if they were to go to a place where there are a few people, their anxiety would spike at first. But if they were to repeat that interaction daily, eventually the anxiety would diminish. As they get more

221

experience being around strangers without experiencing any negative consequences, their brains learn that those situations are not dangerous after all. The part of the brain that has learned to be vigilant learns that it is okay to relax.

Reasonable fear is good

Of course, you want to avoid true danger. If you're afraid of poisonous snakes, wing-suit base jumping, or walking in an unfamiliar part of town after midnight, you may be better off keeping those fears intact. There is, after all, a biological basis for fear, some of which is necessary for survival!

But if your fear is unreasonable, hindering your life or relationships, or adding unfounded anxiety, then it may be time to start dealing with homeopathic doses of safe exposure. If your fear turns into a panic disorder, it's best to meet with a healthcare provider to consider various approaches to treatment.

Premonitions: "I often feel as though something bad is going to happen."

Internalized anxiety

Some people tend to worry and feel anxiety more than others. Often those who frequently feel as though something bad is about to happen grew up in an environment where bad things did occur on a regular basis. These "bad" things aren't necessarily dramatic such as abuse or violence. They could also be more subtle, although also distressing, such as being constantly criticized as a child or having an unstable or unpredictable parent. Sometimes a child is simply internalizing a parent's excessive anxiety.

People growing up in an environment of neglect, abuse, or infectious anxiety may develop a defense system that keeps them on high alert for danger. Their constant vigilance then gets internalized and leads to an ongoing sense of anxiety.

Changing your response

Neuro-plasticity research shows that you can change this high anxiety outlook by replacing each thought with a reasonable substitute.

If you feel that something bad might happen, first check in to see if everything is normal and safe in your current circumstances. You *do* want to protect yourself against obvious danger. Once you see that there is no objective immediate danger, you can consciously replace the worry with a positive thought. For example, replace "What if I get a terrible disease?" with "I will enjoy the health I have right now."

Finally, learn to accept the fact that whatever happens will happen. No one can avoid death. We can take reasonable precautions, but if we spend all our time being wary and worried, we won't have enjoyed the present moments we do have. Thus, there's a certain point at which we have to let go of vigilance and live.

If the negative thought pattern is severe and getting in the way of your wellbeing, a psychotherapist trained in EMDR[6] (Eye movement desensitization and reprocessing) — an often effective treatment for trauma — can often help you change those negative thought patterns.

Catastrophizing: "I failed my test. Now they'll know how stupid I am. I'll never get into college or get a job."

When any small mishap leads you to imagine a downward spiral of horrific consequences, you are likely to become overwhelmed, panicked, or despondent. Moreover, such pessimistic expectations might generate a self-fulfilling prophecy by creating an anxious demeanor. You want to avoid catastrophizing because it is unpleasant, ineffective, and often leads to depression and the deterioration of relationships.

Excessive optimism?

The alternative to pessimism is not a naïve optimism that ignores the challenges of reality. It *is* important to be aware of potential dangers in the world in order to be prepared. We need to strive for a balance between fear and hope, viewing the world with informed awareness.

How do we handle hard times?

When everything seems to be going against us, we need to remember that challenges are part of life and are often merely temporary. The best way to handle difficulties is to face them head on, while maintaining dignity and taking note of the lessons learned.

Black-and-white thinking. *"I used to think she was the best. But now I see she's really evil."*

World of extremes

The flaw behind black-and-white thinking is that it does not reflect the complexity of human nature and the world around us. Most people are not absolutely good or evil. Most events in life have more intricate and varying shades of color.

Black-and–white thinking stems from our reptilian brain, which makes snap decisions as to whether we are safe or in danger in order to help us survive an immediate physical threat. When this ancient part of the brain is triggered, it overrides the reasoning and problem-solving abilities human beings have developed through evolution.

People who were raised to be black-and-white thinkers remain stuck in a world where people and events are viewed in simplistic and extreme terms. Even people who are complex thinkers regress to pigeonholing when they are stressed or overwhelmed by emotion. Unless patterns of fear are counterbalanced, they will prevent people from moving beyond this primitive thinking to more nuanced and sophisticated thinking.

Having a simplistic worldview causes people to suffer unnecessary disappointment, frustration and hurt. For instance, fantasizing about a perfect world with a perfect mate can lead to unrealistic expectations that result in the disappointing conclusion that there are *no* decent men or women out there.

Moreover, having simplistic negative expectations of others tends to bring out their negative traits.

Accepting complexity

Here are some ways to avoid the pitfalls and heartbreaks of black-and-white thinking:

1. Have realistic expectations. Even though optimism generally enhances life, tone down feelings of overblown optimism and unrealistic expectations of specific people or situations.

2. Use words such as "always" and "never" sparingly.

3. Enjoy or at least accept complexity. Beware of considering yourself and others as "the best" or "the worst." The world of absolutes is unrealistic and dull. Find the complexity in any situation or person and you may find what's beautiful or at least interesting.

4. Look for balance. Avoid seeking perfection by accepting the fact that we all make mistakes.

5. Be open to mystery. A curious and open mind embraces mystery without having to put everyone and everything into a box.

It is not the result of scientific research that ennobles humans and enriches their lives, but the struggle to understand while performing creative and open-minded intellectual work.

~Einstein

Red Herring: "That's just the way I am!"

A *red herring* is a verbal ploy to distract a person's attention away from a real issue. It is a tactic used to hide a weakness from the listener by changing the subject. The phrase *red herring* comes from hunting, where the strong scent of herring was used to trick dogs into following the wrong trail. Here's an example of a red herring response to the following request.

"I'd like you to stop being so critical of me; it's really unpleasant."

Red Herring: "It could be a lot worse. At least I don't come home drunk and yell at you."

Instead of addressing the request to stop being critical, the responder simply says, "it could be worse." Well, of course, anything could be worse.

The *ad hominem* attack

One type of red herring is the *ad hominem* — an attack on the speaker rather than a relevant explanation. An *ad hominem* attack feeds the cycle of offense and hurt. Although unproductive, there are some classics that are very witty.

Lady Astor to Churchill: "Sir, you're drunk!"

Winston Churchill: "Yes, Madam. But in the morning, I will be sober and you will still be ugly."

Stay with the issue

The best way to respond to a red herring is to stay focused on the real issue by repeating the question without anger. People who use red herrings a lot generally dread strong reactions, anger, and criticism. They'd rather deflect any uncomfortable questions. So it's important to be persistent without being threatening.

Response to red herring:

A: "Why are you late?"

B: "That's just the way I am!"

A: "That may be the way you are, but I'd still like to know why you're late this time."

227

Response to red herring:

> A: "I'd like you to stop being so critical of me; it's really unpleasant."
>
> B: "It could be a lot worse. At least I don't come home drunk and yell at you."
>
> A: "I'd like you to know how defensive and sad I feel when you're so critical. Would you try to stop criticizing me?"

As for Lady Astor and Churchill, thankfully they didn't resolve their differences. Or we'd miss some great quips.

Lady Astor: "If you were my husband, I'd poison you."
Churchill: "If you were my wife, I'd take it."

---

[1] John B. Arden's *Rewire Your Brain*.
[2] John B. Arden's *Rewire Your Brain*.
[3] Sixty Minutes: *Endless Memory*, December 19, 2010.
[4] David Brooks *The Social Animal*.
[5] John B. Arden's *Rewire your Brain*.
[6] EMDR — Eye Movement Desensitization and Reprocessing Therapy.

8. Money

"Was it stupidity or deliberate dishonesty that caused you to hire your incompetent brother without telling me?"

So what I really meant was...

"I know you want to help your brother, but I'm concerned about our expenses and getting the best quality work we can get. Let's discuss our needs and financial situation together before making promises to other people."

No money: "I get really unhappy not to be able to buy clothes when I see all my friends shopping."

When asked to list their happiest moments, most people will refer to spending time with friends and family, enjoying nature or the arts, accomplishing something difficult, or doing something for a loved one or someone in need.

Few of these pursuits require money. The feeling of enjoyment that comes from learning, accomplishing something, or bringing joy to others lasts longer than simply purchasing new clothes.

There's no denying that buying a new outfit or a new car is pleasurable, and we shouldn't be ashamed of such desires and pleasures. However, such gratification loses its luster very quickly. In fact, that's why many people buy more clothes and stuff than they really need. They have to keep buying more to repeatedly get that quick fix of enjoyment because it fades so quickly.

Instead of focusing on those fleeting highs from getting something new, focus your energy on other more meaningful ways to experience happiness. Then your longing to seek the short-lived gratification of purchasing more stuff is bound to diminish.

Meaningless Consumerism: "I just need one more purse!"

Popular media would have us believe that our loneliness and anxiety are caused by not having enough things or the right kind of stuff. The assumption is that the right stuff will bring us pleasure, friends, love, happiness, and meaning.

Preoccupation with having

While there's nothing inherently bad about desiring material things, *preoccupation* with the acquisition of consumer goods does not satisfy the needs they promise to satisfy. Ironically, a miser is similar to an over-consumer in that they are both preoccupied with material things. The miser clutches fearfully onto resources, while the consumer endlessly acquires and devours more stuff.

> *Consumerism is just the other side of the coin of miserliness. Both are caught by the attempt to take the whole world into their home and to possess it.... And yet, possessing the whole world is equivalent to having nothing at all. The miser and the consumer are fraught with insecurity.*

~Sardello and Severson, "Money & the Soul of the World."

Giving meaning to material things

Rampant consumerism temporarily satiates insatiable yearnings and thereby calms or numbs unwanted anxieties. The problem is that quick-fix consumerism provides only temporary relief and often creates greater cravings.

However, wanting and obtaining material things is not always a symptom of consumerism. Imagine that over the period of a year a child walks by a store window displaying a red bicycle he greatly desires. The child finally receives the bicycle as a gift or saves up to purchase it. That bicycle becomes imbued with much more meaning than if it had been purchased when the child first laid eyes on it.

When we acquire an object very quickly after first desiring it, we don't have time to imagine owning it. So it will not gain as much personal value to us. We start down the path of consumerism when we buy something impulsively without taking the time to consider the acquisition and imagine the satisfaction it might bring us.

Nowadays, many people buy most things soon after they see them. Yet they often discard those same items almost as quickly as they acquire them. When impulse turns into possession too quickly, there's no imagination invested and therefore no time for real desire to develop. As a result, people are unlikely to cherish and take care of the material things they do acquire.

To give meaning to material things and your relationship to them, you need to allow desire to deepen in your imagination through time.

Saving money:
"I want to buy this now!"

It's amazing how fast later comes when you buy now!

~Milton Berle

In baseball, saves are often as important as runs in winning championships. Likewise, saving money is as important as how much money you make.

Yet research shows that when making decisions, most people opt for a small amount of immediate gratification over a larger amount of future gratification. This is because we often make decisions with the emotional rather than the rational part of the brain.

Emotions help us experience and anticipate pleasure and pain. Yet because emotions are stronger when anticipating imminent pleasure or pain, we often give greater weight to instantaneous gratification than to delayed gratification.

So if you want to maximize your happiness, employ your emotions in listing the costs and benefits or pleasure and pain of any purchase. Then take some time using your reason to make an objective decision rather than an impulsive one.

Money can't buy you happiness but it does bring you a more pleasant form of misery.

~Spike Milligan

Dining with Moochers: "I always end up paying for other people when I go out."

Gallantly paying for dinner is an admirable gesture. However, your irritation indicates that you may need to balance your generosity with a little self-preservation.

There are plenty of people who would happily order the best wines at dinner and then allow you to pay for them. Paying for people who repeatedly take advantage of you may result in resentment and financial stress.

Ask yourself whether you feel that your presence is inadequate in itself and that you need to do something extra to be acknowledged and appreciated. When your desire to be appreciated becomes excessive, it becomes self-defeating because you will attract those who will take advantage of you. Generosity is a virtue, but it has to be balanced with other virtues, such as fairness and self-preservation.

So unless you're independently wealthy and enjoy playing to a stream of pandering freeloaders, you may benefit in toning down your magnanimity.

If you go out with people who tend to feel entitled, simply establish ahead of time that you're "going Dutch" so there's no need to worry during dinner. You can ask for a separate check at the beginning of the meal. More importantly, remind yourself that your presence alone is sufficiently valuable.

"I hate my job!"

So what I really meant was...

"It's not my favorite job, but I need the work. So I intend to do it the best I can with the best possible attitude, while looking for a way to transition into something more to my liking."

With this kind of attitude, you'll not only feel satisfaction for a job well done, you may also get promoted or receive a good recommendation when you find work that is more suitable.

No labor, however humble, is dishonoring.

~The Talmud

Financial decisions based on intimidation: "I don't want finances to get in the middle of it because I don't want it to get ugly."

Do not make financial decisions based on fear of a confrontational person (soon-to-be ex, for example.) If you do, then you will remain a victim to intimidating people and situations. It's a law of human nature that manipulative, self-centered people sense when they have the upper hand with those who fear intimidation and confrontation.

Fairness is an appropriate goal. However, *avoiding ugliness* is not. You might be able to avoid friction by being a slave to whatever the confrontational people in your life want, but you cannot control how someone else may react. You certainly would not want to give in to all demands to appease someone's unreasonable behavior.

If you are a person who fears confrontation, your challenges are threefold:

1. to be willing to face another person's unpleasant reactions,

2.   to remain calm and gracious without backing down
        in the face of confrontation, and

3.   to be willing to set up boundaries to enjoy peace and
        harmony.

Remember, *two* people are in charge of finding a peaceful solution — not just one. People are more willing to do what's fair when they know they are not dealing with a pushover.

"I lost my home and job. My life's over."

It's very difficult and frightening to lose what you've worked hard for, particularly your home and your job, and the security that they provide.

Yet what matters most is how you respond to the situation. With courage and a positive attitude and outlook, you are more likely to get back into a situation where you feel comfortable and secure.

I have a friend who lost his beautiful home, all his money, and even his car. In addition to his financial crisis, his marriage fell apart.

Of course he has tremendous regrets about his lost financial security, but his life seems to have changed for the better. With an amazingly positive attitude, he has not dwelled on what could have been.

He's now renting a home, has few expenses, practically no debt, and can live on a lot less money than before. His burden is much lighter than before. He is able to enjoy friends and sports without his previous financial pressures.

My mother too lost her home, as well as friends and family members in WWII Germany, but she did not lose her ability to focus on what she did have — the present moment, the choice to learn and work hard, and most of all, to be grateful for what she did have. With that attitude she became an inspiration to others — another benefit to those who maintain a positive outlook.

"It's unfair that the rich have more fun!"

So what I really meant was...
"I'm going to have more fun!"

"When friends ask me to go out to eat, I'm embarrassed that I can't afford to right now."

Avoid embarrassment

There is no reason to feel embarrassed about making sound financial decisions given your current state of affairs. Many people are in a similar situation. Even in the best of economies, most people have to pay attention to what they spend.

However, if you show embarrassment about your financial difficulties, other people are likely to feel embarrassed for you as well. If you don't act embarrassed, others will feel much more comfortable around you.

See the movie "The Company Men" and notice the attitude of the leading man's wife as she deals with their financial challenges. She employs common sense and a positive attitude, but does not hide behind false pride or shame. Shame or the pretense that "everything's great" when it's not are what prevent real intimacy between friends.

It was once considered a virtue to have good judgment and to refrain from incurring unnecessary expense. Now again, it's becoming embarrassing to flaunt one's money and spend without thinking.

Focus on friendship

The key is to adopt a neutral demeanor, and simply say, "I'd love to get together. But right now, I need to be careful with my spending. Let's have a potluck at my house. Or let's go for a hike."

We can have the most enjoyable times together without spending money. It's the laughter, conversation, and sense of adventure that inspire great moments with our friends.

Look at it as an opportunity to ignite ideas for some special times together that make eating out seem pedestrian!

9. SPORTS

"I don't have any natural talent."

So what I really meant was...

"I can become the best I can be by consistent hard work."

Legendary basketball coach John Wooden said, "Many athletes have tremendous God-given gifts, but they don't focus on the development of those gifts. Who are these individuals? You've never heard of them — and you never will."

Passion, persistence, and hard work make the difference. The discipline to work tenaciously with focused attention amount to much more over the long run than natural talent.

> *There is no such thing as a great talent without great willpower.*
>
> ~Honore de Balzac

Developing New Habits:
"I never exercise the way I should. I went to the gym twice and then gave up."

Changing habits is difficult, but it can be done. Research shows that people who are successful in developing new habits, such as exercising more, tend to apply the following guidelines to motivate themselves[1]:

1.   Focus on pleasure. Frame your new habit in terms of what will give you pleasure. Remind yourself that

you're choosing a healthy lifestyle, which is more pleasurable than one of inactivity. Choose a sport or exercise that interests you or that will bring you joy. Don't go to the gym if you'd rather go on a walk, a hike, or a bike-ride outdoors. Figure out a way to enjoy the activity, such as doing it to music or with a friend.

2. Make a step-by-step plan. Having a series of intermediate goals rather than one over-arching goal diminishes your fear of failure and the magnitude of the goal. Each goal should be attainable and within easy reach.

3. Consistency is key. You're more likely to be consistent if you have realistic expectations of yourself. For example, start with a minimum of five or ten minutes of exercise a day, though you might aspire to an hour a day. You're more likely to develop a new habit if your goals are achievable. Starting is the hard part. Once you start walking or swimming and enjoying it, it's easier to stay out longer and you are likely to continue. If you take a class or schedule regular exercise routines with a friend you are more likely to follow through consistently.

4. Reflect on regrets and benefits. Think of how much you'll regret it if you don't exercise. Research shows that a few moments of reflecting on potential regret will motivate a person to get started.

5. Tell your family and friends. Telling others of your goals helps motivate you to achieve them and might encourage them to participate. When you state your goals publicly, you increase your motivation to live up to them, and you garner the support of others.

6. Reward yourself. Be grateful for every step you take and give yourself a reward for every intermediate goal achieved.

Exercise becomes easier the more you pursue it because it triggers mood-enhancing endorphins that give you more energy, health, and vitality, making it increasingly desirable in itself.

GOALS: "I really want to win, but I never do."

To set an appropriate goal, you need to be clear about what it will accomplish for you in your life. If your goal is limited to proving to yourself or others that you are superior, then you're likely to be frustrated, unhappy, and miss out on other types of enjoyment — whether or not you achieve your goal.

When you can broaden the reasons for which you pursue a sport, you are more likely to enjoy it, improve at it, and to hang in there through the challenging times. It's helpful to expand and appreciate the many reasons for which you can pursue a sport.

What to appreciate in a sport

- The exercise
- The adventure
- The camaraderie
- The beautiful environment
- The challenge of improving your results in competition
- The challenge of strategizing your game plan
- The sense of accomplishment after hard work and practice
- The occasional timeless feeling of being in the zone
- The enjoyment of the physical feeling of a clean move

- The thrill of speed

The more reasons you have for pursuing a sport the better. If you have a competitive goal, whether it's going for a world record or your personal best for this season, enjoying the many other facets of a sport helps buoy you in times of challenge and defeat.

Sportsmanship: "That referee's an idiot."

I never thought about losing, but now that it's happened, the only thing is to do it right.

~ Muhammad Ali

The most inspirational moment at the 2011 National Water Ski Championships for me was seeing a top-seeded Men's Slalom skier display amazing sportsmanship after having his entry gates called on his first pass. Rather than raging or complaining, he shrugged it off, but determined to do better next time.

That's not to say that he isn't very competitive and didn't really want to win the tournament. But once the call was made, he was able to handle himself with integrity, rather than display feelings of defeat and aggravation — and this at the age of 20!

To me, this young man's ability to maintain perspective about his performance was at least as impressive as the 180-foot water-ski jumps and multiple back-flip trick runs exhibited at the site.

I've missed more than 9,000 shots in my career, lost almost 300 games, missed the game-winning shot 26 times. I've failed over and over again in my life. That is why I succeed.

~ Michael Jordan

ATTITUDE: "I'm so nervous about blowing it again."

Our physical attitude usually reflects our mental attitude. Our bodies perform best when we are both relaxed and intently focused in the moment. Therefore, a mental attitude that promotes fluidity and power is optimal. Strong negative emotions can cause your muscles to stiffen. So, deal with errors without becoming frustrated.

Look at the attitude of young children when they learn to walk. They observe and practice. When they fall down, they get right back up and keep trying, taking physical or mental note on what worked and what did not. The best learning occurs without whining or outbursts, but through calm awareness and perseverance.

TRAINING: "It's just practice. So I don't really care how I play."

Observe other athletes whom you would like to emulate. Visualize and imagine yourself doing the appropriate moves well. Get good coaching. Understanding your sport well will help you get out of a slump more quickly and enable you to self-correct during training.

Focus on the moment and learn coping skills to deal with distractions during your practice. Water ski world record holder Chris Parish's father would shoot paintballs at him during practice while Slalom Champion Jamie Beauchesne's dad would drive the boat around to make the water rough for practice. Both Chris and Jamie learned to handle distractions without losing their focus.

Finally, it always helps to be grateful for the chance to practice the sport, especially if no one's shooting paintballs at you.

GAME DAY: "It's pretty cold and windy today; I don't feel like going because I'll probably blow it."

Keep your focus in the present instead of thinking about the result you want or worrying about failure. Focusing on the present moment during every practice trains the brain to keep that kind of focus in competition.

Some people who are generally consistent with their performance have problems during competition because of their emotions and nerves. It helps to conjure up nerves during practice by imagining that you're in a competition. It also helps to use imagery to see yourself performing well under pressure.

Mix it up in training to evoke excitement and nerves. For example, do your sport in a variety of settings, in difficult conditions, and with different people. However, there is nothing that beats getting used to the pressure of competition than competing in many events.

"I'm terrible at this sport. I will never get it right."

The problems with self-denigration

Swearing, throwing your equipment, and beating yourself up mentally will not inspire you to improve at any sport. Being hard on yourself simply doesn't put you in the right frame of mind to progress.

Maintaining some humility gives a person perspective. But don't let modesty turn into self-ridicule. Endless negative comments about how inept you are takes away from focusing on the goals you set *and* it's annoying to those around you.

It's difficult to be around people who moan, sigh, and complain about how lame they are. The fact is most people focus more on their own game than how others are doing. However, what people do notice is other people's attitude. If you're struggling, there's no need to showcase your frustration. It's important to maintain both your game-face and perspective.

Focus on what you need to do

To improve at a sport and be able to enjoy it, you need to stay cool and focused. No matter what your level, it does not help to dwell on feeling disappointed about your performance. Simply focus on what you need to do to get better. Then practice, and practice some more.

Enhancing your game requires constructive analysis, coaching, focus, and practice. Constructive analysis means figuring out what you're doing right and what you could do to improve without getting emotional.

The ideal mental and physical attitude for improving your game incorporates both intense focus and relaxed flexibility — which in turn is a good approach for living your life.

Being Chicked: "I hate it when my girlfriend beats me."

I am in a great relationship with a wonderful woman. We have many interests in common and we love participating in sports (running, skiing, biking) together. Unfortunately, I get "chicked" by my girlfriend a lot. When she beats me in a race, I tend to get distant with her. I want her to accomplish her goals, but how do I balance her lofty achievements against my own self-esteem? Sincerely,

Bruised ego

Self-esteem

Having mixed feelings about self-esteem, relationships, and competition reflects the complexity of those issues within each of us. People sometimes feel they can be valued or esteemed only when they surpass their partner in certain arenas. Interestingly, in some cultures there is little notion of self-esteem. Instead, people are concerned with group identity and their role within the group.

Today's Western culture, however, promotes a view of self-esteem based on individual success. Children are raised getting extensive praise for excelling, winning competitions, or standing out as being special. Ironically, excessive focus on outshining others to increase self-esteem often leads people to depend on external validation to feel good. When people don't win or stand out, they may feel empty and inadequate, which leads to feeling distant and detached from those around them. Thus, the way we tend to instill self-esteem can be self-defeating, because it encourages dependence on others for a sense of self-worth.

Being Special[2]

Somebody who finds it crucial to be "special" tends to feel vulnerable when not being admired for being the best, the smartest, the most beautiful, the most skillful, or unique. When we feel vulnerable, it's easy to blame either others or ourselves for our discomfort, and this creates new problems.

A need for continuous praise also makes it difficult to relax and enjoy other meaningful parts of life. Exclusive focus on being special can foster paradoxical results — ambition and success on the one hand, depression and unhappiness on the other.

Here's the key: *Praise and criticism are excessive when there's little concern about how the individual actually experiences life.*

Being Ordinary

We spend much of our lives being ordinary and doing ordinary things, many of which can give us much meaning and pleasure. Ordinary enjoyment arises simply from doing and being, rather than from external validation. There can be great fulfillment in bike riding, gardening, playing with your kids, talking with a stranger, or reading a good book. When you focus on your own experience of life and your connection with others, something ineffable about who you are shines through your activities, which has nothing to do with being better than others.

What is self-worth based on?

Let's take a closer look at the various sources of meaning and enjoyment so we can reconfigure our sense of self-worth. A bike competition is a good example of an event that can encompass many different layers of meaning as well as enjoyment. For example, consider

- the personal enjoyment of the ride,
- the personal feeling of competence,
- participation with people who have the same passion,
- sharing the experience with a partner or friend, which adds a new dimension to the relationship and a shared history,
- the adventure of humor of the mishaps,
- the excitement of being in a competition and the risk of winning or losing,
- admiration from others for doing well, and
- admiration for those who do even better.

When we appreciate more layers of enjoyment in competitions and elsewhere in life, our enjoyment becomes richer and less vulnerable to "defeat." When we merely focus on one aspect, we miss out on all the other meaningful facets. If we only value beating others in competition — or being admired by others — we'll be disappointed often, particularly as we age. Most gold medalists and prizefighters end up having to learn that lesson later in life and many never come to terms with it. Some end up living in the past, trying to recapture the rapture of those special moments.

Ideally, you would balance the feeling of being "chicked" with all the other aspects of the ride. For instance, you could balance your disappointment about not winning with your enjoyment of the bike ride and the sense of community in participating in the race. You might also find joy and pride in your girlfriend's achievement.

Couples who polarize

No two people are alike. Often in a relationship, one of the partners has a more noticeably "special" quality. When one partner is known as the well-known artist or a great mountain bike rider, for example, the other has the option to rejoice in that success or to feel left behind. The feeling of being left behind can polarize the couple, exacerbating feelings of inadequacy and creating distance in the relationship.

In many places in the world and in our recent past, men had a superior role in the relationship especially in sports and the workplace, while women were expected to play a subservient role. In the last fifty years we have moved away from this split in roles. This is fortunate for both men and women. When someone purposely diminishes him- or herself to allow another to feel superior, it implies that the other person's ego is fragile and dependent on being dominant in the relationship.

As an example, think of the many older men in the past who become despondent after retirement due to feelings of worthlessness. When self-worth is dependent on feelings of superiority, a person misses the chance to experience life through expressing and interacting through his or her authentic self.

To Bruised Ego

The discomfort you feel when your girlfriend excels may be a residual reaction cultivated by our culture or your upbringing. Some people feel dejected whenever someone beats them in a competition; others react this way only when a woman surpasses them. The very fact that you are grappling with your feelings of self-esteem allows you to make a conscious decision in how to react rather than to merely react impulsively according to your current emotion. As you focus on a more multi-faceted experience of enjoyment and meaning, your feelings of unease will diminish.

The fact that your girlfriend does not play down her abilities indicates that she has faith that you have adequate self-respect and that your self-worth is not dependent on your bike riding skills. When you look at it this way, you might find it inspiring to have a partner who sees your inner character rather than simply your biking prowess. I'm sure it is also inspiring for her to be with a partner who supports her aspirations and appreciates her competitive spirit.

---

[1] Richard Wiseman's *59 Seconds*.
[2] Read Hal and Sidra Stone's *Embracing Our Selves*.

10. ATTITUDE

"I hate Mondays!"

So what I really meant was...

"Perspective changes everything. I'm going to stop complaining, change my attitude, and see what happens."

I had no shoes and complained, until I met a man who had no feet.

~Indian Proverb

Negative Assumptions:
"He didn't acknowledge me. He must not like me."

So what I really meant was...

"He was probably upset, preoccupied, or rushed because of something else. It has nothing to do with me."

We rarely know what others are thinking. So don't take things personally.

Your preconceptions about other people can and will influence how they feel about you and about themselves. So don't assume the worst. If the behavior continues, ask if he's all right or if there is something upsetting him.

If he really doesn't like you, don't dwell on it. Reconsider your expectations of your relationship with him and focus on the people you get along with better.

Embarrassing Relatives: "Can't you chew with your mouth closed!!"

Embarrassment makes it worse

Everyone has some relative who has bad table manners, belongs to a crazy cult, or drinks too much. We tend to be hardest on those closest to us. We are easily embarrassed by them and want desperately to eradicate their bad habits. Ironically, however, when we show embarrassment and disapproval, we tend to highlight the situation and draw out the worst in those around us. Moreover, it's unappealing to care more about the family image than about our treatment of family members.

Our relatives don't define who we are. Besides, no one is perfect. Life is too short to agonize about the imperfections in those around us. Often, a sense of humor can help us overlook our family's extreme political views or incessant bragging.

You're usually better off not trying to change adult relatives. If they haven't changed in 20 years, they are not likely to see the light now. The exception would be if they became deeply motivated to change within themselves and seek your input.

Abusive behavior

Abusive behavior or language, however, is another matter completely. It's important to speak up or leave when someone is aggressive or acts inappropriately, for example, in the case of name-calling, abusive criticism, or violence. When responding to a verbal attack, you could say, "Calling me names is denigrating to both of us, and makes me want to leave. If you have something to say to me, let's talk about it in private." If they can't stop their belittling behavior, then it's time to limit or stop spending your time with mean-spirited or abusive relatives.

Harmless personality quirks, however, are better seen as a source of amusement rather than providing you with a mission to improve others. Challenge yourself to use your wit, creativity, and humanity to overlook imperfections and to bring out the best in those eccentric family members around you.

You're only given a little spark of madness. You mustn't lose it.

~Robin Williams

"Why did she give me that gift? She knows I hate red."

So what I really meant was...

"It's the thought that counts. If I can't exchange it, I'll be ready for the next white elephant party."

A wise lover values not so much the gift of the lover as the love of the giver.

~Thomas á Kempis

"How could she do that to me?"

Disappointment as a signal

Disappointment is the feeling of unhappiness, which result from your expectations not being realized. You feel let down due to the belief that you're going to miss out on something forever.

All feelings have a purpose. Disappointment calls on you to modify your behavior or your thinking. It is often a sign that you need to change your expectations, actions, or relationships to effectively take into account your experience.

If you figure out what you can learn from your experience and change your expectations, then you can move on rather than linger in the frustration that disappointment inevitably triggers. Once you've assessed why your expectations were unrealistic, you might be able to avoid repeating similar mistakes in the future.

However, don't expect to avoid disappointment in the future. In order to do that, you'd have to give up all of your hopes, dreams, and expectations. Life would become dull and lifeless. A fulfilling life entails dreams and expectations, as well as frustrations and disappointments.

Two common mistakes to avoid:

1. Dwelling on the disappointment, and
2. Avoiding future disappointment by becoming cynical or reclusive.

An old Chinese tale shows how apparent misfortune can turn out to be good fortune and vice versa.

The son of a farmer had captured several fine wild horses. The neighbors were envious and murmured about his good luck. But the farmer shrugged his shoulders — "Life has its ups and downs," he said. A few days later, the son broke his leg when trying to tame one of the horses. This time the neighbors whispered about his bad luck, but the farmer just shrugged his shoulders.

Another week went by and government agents came by and took along every able-bodied man to fight invaders. The farmer's son stayed behind.

Change

Disappointment can lead to positive and healthy changes. It can cause you to re-evaluate what you desire and pursue. Disappointment can spark desirable improvement in a relationship or in some cases a necessary dissolution. It can help you to set new goals and expectations on a continuous basis.

Twenty years from now you will be more disappointed by the things that you didn't try than by the ones you did. So throw off the bowlines. Sail away from the safe harbor. Catch the trade winds in your sails. Explore. Dream. And discover.

"What is there to be cheerful about?"

Cheerfulness is a powerful emotion. It is similar to gratitude, yet its perspective is more forward looking. A cheerful approach to life entails a can-do attitude of making the most of what happens in your life. Its positive effect on the quality of your life and those around you cannot be overestimated. More and more research shows that cheerfulness materially changes brain chemistry and helps enhance mental and physical health.

Being cheerful, however, does not entail bubbly naïveté or refusal to acknowledge life's difficulties. Pollyanna cheerfulness can be false and annoying. There is an important place for painful emotions.

No matter what struggles you face, you can still develop a cheerful attitude. An attitude of cheerfulness means being willing to take on life's challenges instead of sitting back and complaining about them. This does not mean that you don't feel pain or are not aware of the challenges that exist. It means that you are willing to embrace the positive expectation that you can overcome such challenges, and in doing so, you powerfully impact your life and relationships.

"Why do you always contradict me when I tell a story? Besides you're wrong!"

So what I really meant was…

"Now don't let the truth get in the way of a good story!"

People often like to correct their family members in the middle of their telling a story. Unless the correction is critical to the story and given respectfully, those literalists usually just cause embarrassment and bickering.

So don't get drawn in. Keep a sense of humor, and calmly continue the story.

"WHO tracked all this mud into the house?! How thoughtless!"

Assigning blame does not fix a wrong or prevent it from happening in the future. It only causes people to feel defensive.

Being able to speak up and ask people to do things differently and to ask for help without blaming is absolutely key to improving day-to-day life and relationships.

Fixing not Blaming

Focus on cleaning up, not on *who* made a mess. When people know you are not going to blame them, they will feel better about fixing the problem. People prefer to get praised for doing the right thing than chastised for making mistakes.

Ask for help in an upbeat way. Here are some examples:

- "I'd love to get some help cleaning up this mud."
- "It doesn't matter who did this. What matters is who will help clean it up."
- "Please help me put this right."

When dealing with young children, ask *them* how to best avoid the situation in the future. For instance, ask how tracking mud into the house can be avoided. It helps when they make the observation themselves, and they usually know the answer.

However, don't quiz an adult. You don't want to get into a parent/child relationship with an adult. It's better to simply ask for help.

If you don't speak up at all, you'll become resentful and you'll be dealing with a lot of mud in the house and other things that annoy you. Moreover, the perpetrator will have little respect for you.

"I feel drained after hanging out with someone so negative."

So what I really meant was...

"I'm going to spend time with people who enrich my life."

Time is valuable. The people you spend time with have a big impact on your life. It's important to choose people, activities, and books that elevate your thinking, your attitude, and your life.

You are the average of the 5 people you spend the most time with.

~Jim Rohn

"The world is deteriorating. Where's the opportunity?"

A pessimist sees the difficulty in every opportunity; an optimist sees the opportunity in every difficulty.

~Winston Churchill

Realistic optimism, that is, hopefulness and confidence about the future with clear understanding of a given reality, enhances quality of life and longevity. Optimism requires us to intentionally seek opportunity, beauty, and possibility, even in circumstances that don't seem to hold out much hope, as in the following example:

A pessimist was sitting in a room full of toys and he did nothing but whine and cry. In contrast, the optimist was placed in a room full of horse manure and given a shovel. The optimist was happily shoveling away the manure. When asked why she was so happy, she said: "There's got to be a pony in here somewhere!"

"I'm stuck. I'm waiting for some inspiration."

Why wait for inspiration? It may never come. In any event, it comes more often to people who persevere at working hard. Such people count on perspiration not inspiration. They don't want to be at the whim of so elusive a visitor.

In Carlos Ruiz Zafon's novel *The Angel's Game*, the protagonist writer David Martin says the following about waiting for inspiration:

Inspiration comes when you stick your elbows on the table and your bottom on the chair and start sweating. Choose a theme, an idea, and squeeze your brain until it hurts. That's called inspiration.

"I'm tired of my wife telling me to use my knife instead of my finger to push food on my fork."

Good manners are made up of petty sacrifices.

~Ralph Waldo Emerson

So what I really meant was…

"I might as well use my knife. It's not worth fighting over. That's a pretty easy way to make her happy, and I'll have decent table manners too."

On the other hand, if her criticism of you is excessive, you might quote the following:

The test of good manners is to be patient with bad ones.

~Gabirol, *The Choice of Pearls*

Regret: "I'm an idiot for yelling at my friend."

Pangs of regret poison your ability to learn from mistakes as well as your ability to move on and enjoy life. Even if you have a legitimate regret, the best approach is to take note of your regret, learn from your mistake, and then to let it go.

Here are three questions to ask yourself when you feel regret:

1. What can I do now to improve the situation? Can I apologize or take some action to mitigate the consequences?

2. How can I reframe the situation to try to get something positive out of it?

3. What can I do in the future to handle a similar situation better? If I do not learn from this lesson, I am bound to repeat it — to my later regret.

For example, if you regret having yelled at your friend, consider the following steps:

1. Apologize. Explain what happened. For instance, you might say, "I don't usually speak up for myself, but when I do, I tend to do it more harshly than necessary. I'm sorry."

2. Recognize that you need to stand up for yourself more tactfully without yelling.

3. Speak up *earlier* and be diplomatic about it, instead of waiting until you're so fed up that you lose your temper.

> *When one door closes, another opens; but we often look so long and so regretfully upon the closed door that we do not see the one which has opened for us.*
>
> ~Alexander Graham Bell

"Aaarghh! I've got crow's feet — I look terrible!"

So what I really meant was...

"What matters most is how I feel, not how I look. What matters is how I behave in the world and how I pursue my relationships, my passions, and my work."

Most people prefer spending time with those who exude vitality over those who look young but are vain and self-absorbed.

> *Your wrinkles either show that you're nasty, cranky, and senile, or that you're often smiling.*
>
> ~Carlos Santana

"I am so unlucky."

If you want to be lucky, there are a few things you can do to entice luck to your side. Research shows that lucky people are more relaxed and open than unlucky people.[1]

Being more relaxed and open leads to the following essentials for good luck:

1. Awareness and curiosity: Being relaxed and open to new possibilities allows a person to recognize chance opportunities, and then act on them. When you are overly anxious and concerned with doing things just right, you limit your ability to notice people and opportunities around you.

2. Approachability: Luck often originates from random encounters with other people, and being relaxed makes a person more approachable and easy to talk to about new ideas.

3. Flexibility: Being reasonably relaxed often leads to varied and flexible life experiences. Open-mindedness and receptivity to wide-ranging experiences and diverse people in your life fosters creativity. On the other hand,

trying too hard, being particular, and emphasizing perfection can lead to being inflexible.

Curiosity, approachability, and flexibility lead away from narrow-mindedness. They allow a person to talk to a wide range of people and to have a spirit of adventure when life doesn't go as expected.

There is more to being lucky than being relaxed and open. Knowledge, preparedness, experience, and hard work can transform luck to success. However, the qualities of being relaxed and open are key to finding opportunities and allowing for creative thinking, which can turn incidental events into serendipitous good-fortune.

"I hate being so fearful."

Fear is a signal

Fear is an emotional response that alerts you to potential danger like a car's warning light. Without a warning, you could get into deep trouble.

On the other hand, if that warning light is as loud as a security alarm system that screeches "INTRUDER! INTRUDER!" it will scare the daylights out of you. Being overcome by fear can cause mental paralysis and panic, and makes it difficult to deal with situations in a rational manner.

It's more effective to treat fear as an indicator telling you to be alert and to look at your situation with an eye toward short- and long-term consequences. Obviously, if the danger is a life-and-death matter like a child running into the street, then you must act quickly in defense of the child. But in most cases we can take time to resolve things that we fear.

Responses to fear

1. With a pen in hand and the serenity prayer[2] in mind, figure out what you have control over.
2. Look rationally at your priorities and carefully weigh the pros and cons.
3. Be creative and imagine various possible actions you could take.
4. Figure out and take the appropriate first step.
5. Imagine what the worst possible outcome could be. Recognize that it will probably not be as bad as you imagine.

Once you start creatively listing potential actions and thoughtfully analyzing those choices, you have engaged other parts of your mind. Engaging the rational part of your mind will help alleviate the panic, choose a course of action, and avert or minimize any potential danger.

"I am such a loser. I blew it."

So what I really meant was...

"I can't change the past, but I can control my attitude and learn from my mistakes."

"I'm bored."

Boredom flourishes too, when you feel safe. It's a symptom of security.

~Eugene Ionesco

Fear of emptiness

Boredom is a sense of suspension in moments that lack purpose, intensity, and activity. Boredom can arise when life is safe and easy and a person lacks challenge, motivation, and curiosity. People who are driven to experience lively engagement of their minds and bodies may feel uncomfortable when they temporarily lack direction and stimulation.

Someone who is bored might seek entertainment either to feed self-centeredness or to avoid self-reflection, which are two sides of the same coin. Boredom is often caused by the anxiety of having to face the emptiness that underlies quiet moments. It may conceal an unconscious fear that there will be nothing to feel if one is not active, excited, or busy.

To avoid falling into a disconnected limbo, there are many quick fixes. Technological games, comfort foods, and constant connectivity are easy distractions but don't amount to a deep engagement of the mind and body.

Creativity and depth

On the other hand, persevering through boredom without seeking distraction can lead to self-awareness, self-reflection, and groundedness. As a result, creativity will often blossom.

People sometimes say, "If you're bored, you lack imagination." Perhaps it's the other way around: *creative imagination requires the ability to withstand stillness.* Creativity, where two unconnected ideas collide to create a new idea, occurs when the mind is relaxed and aware, but not overly distracted. Sometimes texting, computer games, web surfing, and looking in the refrigerator allow for free flow movement and the deepening of ideas, but sometimes they are simply mind-numbing activities.

What to do when you're bored

1. **Sit with the boredom.** Mathematician and inventor Pascal wrote, "All man's troubles come from not knowing how

to sit still in one room." By occasionally avoiding distractions one is able to observe what lies underneath the unease caused by boredom. Rather than reaching for your cell, the TV remote, or a bag of chips to kill the boredom, use the time to sit or take a walk and "be with" yourself.

2. **Focus on other people.** Helping someone else instantly frees a person from the weariness of boredom. Rather than thinking about how to entertain yourself, think about how you could brighten someone else's day. Volunteer work, for example, with the intent to help others is gratifying and absorbing. Even smiling at or making a fleeting connection with strangers can make a difference to you and the other person.

3. **Work or study.** Excessive work and study can be used to busy oneself and hide from reality. But mindful work or study is often a way to avoid the pitfalls of self-indulgence and self-pity. Dale Carnegie once recommended, "Are you bored with life? Then throw yourself into some work you believe in with all your heart, live for it, die for it, and you will find happiness that you had thought could never be yours."

If boredom is an ongoing theme in your life, it may be helpful to find work or enroll in classes to help you participate in the world in a more meaningful way. Many people do better with external motivation, which school and work provide, directing their focus on something other than their own vague yearnings and discontent.

"Oh no! Now there's broken glass all over! You're so clumsy!"

So what I really meant was…
"Don't worry. Let's get the broom."

"Don't you love me?"

Yearning and neediness

The question "Don't you love me?" sounds needy and weak. You'll probably get a "Yes, of course I do," but it won't be very satisfying, because the yearning behind the question carries an element of coercion. There's a sense of "You better answer 'yes', because if you don't soothe my doubts, I'll fall apart and then you'll really have to take care of me."

No one likes to be coerced. It's human nature to be put off by neediness. Ironically, the very people who want so much to be desired and loved cause others to lose desire for them by their desperate craving.

Self-acceptance and validation

Instead of pressuring someone to validate you, it's healthier to accept and validate yourself. It takes willpower, self-awareness, and a lot of practice to stand on your own. While it may be difficult to resist asking for validation and love, it will make you stronger as well as more desirable to others, and thus, more likely to get the love you crave.

If you have to ask, then at least say, "I know you're crazy about me," or "Tell me all the reasons you love me," but say it with confidence and a smile in your eyes.

This is not to say that you shouldn't ask for affection or support in a difficult time. Beware, however, of turning every moment of slight insecurity into a swamp of self-doubt that will require someone to dig you out and prop you up.

"Oh NO! Not another problem!"

So what I really meant was...

"How much will this matter in two weeks or a year from now?"

Keep things in perspective.

Focus on those situations over which you have control. Look at the whole situation you're dealing with, and then figure out what is the most critical thing you should attend to first. Manage the situation one feasible step at a time.

> *The older I get the more wisdom I find in the ancient rule of taking first things first. A process which often reduces the most complex human problem to a manageable proportion.*
>
> ~Dwight D. Eisenhower

"I've fallen out of love."

Love as Action, not just Feeling

It's important for couples to talk about work, parenting, money issues, and the practicalities of life. Yet it is also important for couples to spend time together simply enjoying each other's company as they did when they first met.

267

Deliberately Romantic

The busyness of life, particularly when there are children, makes it difficult to deliberately make time to relish being together without a particular agenda or purpose. When you spend all day being a responsible parent, planning schedules, giving advice, or dealing with controversies at work, it takes deliberate intention to switch into a connecting, fun-loving, or romantic mode.

Co-parents and Roommates

If a conscious choice isn't made to enjoy each other, then couples tend to relate to each other as responsible parents or roommates, which doesn't do much for the magic in a relationship. The romance will fade rapidly.

The reason divorce rates are so high when children leave home for college or work is that many couples don't sustain their relationship as couples, but get in the habit of relating to each other primarily as co-parents, co-workers, or cohabitants. As a result, the powers of attraction and energetic connection have been left to wither in the cold. When the children leave home or life becomes less busy, the void and the longing for passion become conspicuously noticeable.

Love as a Feeling

People complain that they've fallen out of love as though they have had no choice about the matter. Love is often viewed as a feeling. However, love actually involves more than just fleeting feelings that randomly come and go. Love requires action over which we do have control. There *is* something we can do to sustain love in a relationship.

Falling in Love

When we fall in love, we get a feeling of wholeness. We generally fall in love with someone who carries some qualities we lack in ourselves and that the beloved carries in an attractive way.

When we first fall in love, we're in a state of awe and wonder, which inspires our partner to feel confident and open — two appealing qualities.

Falling out of Love

Later in a relationship, the very qualities we fell in love with in our partner often drive us crazy. The irony is that the more we criticize and try to change our partner, the less our partner will change, and the more we get annoyed.

We may also fall out of love because we no longer bring the fun-loving, romantic, and new creative energy to the relationship. When we stop being passionate about life, appreciative of our partners, and developing ourselves, it negatively affects the way we feel about those around us.

Love as an Chosen Attitude

In contrast, the more we appreciate our partner, the more he or she will carry those opposing qualities in an attractive way, and thus, the more likely we are to get that loving feeling. It all starts with our own conscious choice to appreciate the differences without denigrating either ourselves or our partner. The act of loving someone after the initial dopamine cocktail wears off involves choosing to have an attitude of appreciation and making an effort to be a well-rounded person who is enjoyable to be with as well.

Practical steps to promote the love and happiness between a couple include taking some time together, whether it's 20 minutes a day or an afternoon a week, to have fun, be romantic, listen to music, or have an adventure. To sustain a loving relationship, couples should consciously invite the spirit of awe, adventure, appreciation, and mystery into the relationship on a regular basis.

---

[1] Richard Wiseman's *The Luck Factor*.

2 The Serenity Prayer:

> *God grant me the serenity to accept the things I cannot change;*
> *The courage to change the things I can;*
> *and the wisdom to know the difference.*
> *Living one day at a time;*
> *Enjoying one moment at a time;*
> *Accepting hardships as the pathway to peace....*

11. HAPPINESS

"I need to eliminate all stress from my life."

Is it healthier to have stress or no stress in your life?

It depends.

Control

Most people would imagine that their wellbeing improves as stress in their life diminishes. However, studies about stress and happiness are complex and do not necessarily conclude what you would imagine. Research found clear signs of accelerated aging in those who reported the least control over their lives.[1] However, longevity and wellbeing tend to be greater for those *with* stress in their lives *when they have some control* over their lives. In other words some stress can be a good thing!

Surprisingly, you tend to live the longest, feel the happiest, and have the strongest immune system when you *do* have stress as long as you *also* feel that you have some control over those stressful situations in your life. In fact, if you have some control rather than being powerless, then stress is healthier than if you have practically no stress at all.

Cortisol

Stress causes the production of cortisol, and having too little cortisol can be just as unhealthy as having too much. Active participation in directing your life with its inherent difficulties turns out to be better than passive acceptance of an easy life or helplessness in face of a difficult life.

271

Life is rarely stress-free because it requires us to deal with the unknown. The more practice we get in handling the unknown, the more confidently we can approach life. The same holds true for hardships; the more actively we endeavor to handle difficulties, the greater our ability to take appropriate action in the future.

Take Action

A good anti-aging and happiness tip, therefore, is to focus primarily on problems you can do something about. Taking control requires taking positive steps to deal with challenges, rather than ignoring them and suppressing the resulting stress.

Such steps might include prioritizing situations in your life, changing your situation, and adjusting your perspective. Just as important in striving for happiness is relieving your tension in healthy ways such as exercising, laughing, and relaxing with friends or family. In cases where you can't take physical action, you can take action by consciously adjusting your attitude and thinking about any given situation. Put things in perspective.

The violin makes its most beautiful resonance when its strings are under enough tension.

~Charlie Stuart

"All I want is a Lamborghini. Then I'd be happy!"

The meaning of fantasy

Fantasies reveal to us symbolically what we may be missing in our lives. When we look at our fantasies metaphorically, they can point the way to our finding wholeness. However, we often take them too literally and fail to realize the real need underlying the fantasy. For instance, the desire for an exceptional car might really signify our need for personal power, freedom, or a sense of being special.

Indulging literally in the whims of imagination can be a pleasurable escape from everyday reality. It can also inspire you to work hard, to pursue a new path, and even to change the course of your life. However, fantasies are deceptive in that they highlight the pleasure, thrill, and magic of what's possible, and leave out the dreary, difficult, and inconvenient aspects of the reality of getting there. They often substitute the literal object for the quality that we could benefit from developing in ourselves.

Lottery winners

Statistics have shown that most lottery winners lose all their gains within five years and often wish they had never won the lottery. The documentary film *Lucky* follows several lottery winners to see how their "luck" ends up changing their lives.

One of the few people whose life was not spoiled by winning the lottery was a math professor who had always fantasized about buying a Lamborghini. Once he was able to make his fantasy a reality, however, he chose not to buy the exotic car, but to stick with his car and his life because he realized that the fantasy was better than the would-be reality. He decided that owning the car would not be worth the envy of his neighbors nor the worry about where to safely park the precious car.

Making fantasy reality

I am not implying that it might not be satisfying to acquire exceptional things. It's simply wise to remember that fantasies don't take into consideration the various challenges and burdens that come with their realization. Besides, whatever fantasies come true, you will probably remain the same person.

On the other hand, when you recognize what is motivating your fantasy, you don't have to win the lottery to start integrating the sought-after qualities within yourself. You can develop personal power and freedom without having a special car to show for it.

"My life has no purpose or meaning."

Once people have good health and the necessities of life, it's natural to pursue greater challenges, pleasure, excitement, or purpose.

Now and then it's helpful to pause and consider what has been most fulfilling and meaningful in our lives. Many people find that they were most fulfilled during challenging times pursuing difficult goals or meeting great challenges. Others find the times where they helped or gave to others are near the top of the list.

Contributing to others enhances not only other people's lives, but is one of the best ways to enhance your own. It is wonderful to know that the way you've lived your life and how you've treated others has positively affected other people. Knowing that your actions or words have contributed to someone else's wellbeing is very gratifying.

Not everyone has the time or resources to contribute to others in a consistent or large-scale way by doing volunteer work or making donations. This, however, does not exclude you from developing a giving nature. Giving to others can include small kindnesses such as a warm smile, sincere compliments, and encouraging words. Contributing to others may simply mean bringing the best of yourself to those with whom you interact.

There is no requirement that you directly serve others if you are not drawn to service. Being a role model in terms of your work ethic, your relationships, or your ability to enjoy life can also enhance other people's lives and give your own life meaning and purpose.

"I don't know what will make me happy."

The very fact that we spend time thinking about happiness is one good reason to be happy. The mere consideration of how to pursue happiness implies that we enjoy a backdrop of freedom from oppression and deprivation.

One of the most powerful statements in the United States' founding documents shows the connection between equality and the pursuit of happiness:

> *We hold these truths to be self-evident, that all men are created equal, that they are endowed by their Creator with certain unalienable Rights, that among these are Life, Liberty and the pursuit of Happiness.*
>
> ~ *The Declaration of Independence*

Sadly, in too many countries people do not have the luxury of discussing happiness because the political environment does not allow the freedom needed to make meaningful choices. Poverty combined with a totalitarian regime oppresses people to the point where mere survival is all that they can think about.

We who live in countries that aspire to freedom and equality before the law are very fortunate in being able to have some ability to follow our own path to a happy and meaningful life.

Even if we don't know what will make us happy, we can be grateful that we have enough security in our lives to consider what *might* make us happy.

Perfectionism: "I would like to invite people over but it's stressful to cook a great meal."

If you want to spend time with friends but don't want to work hard preparing a fabulous meal, have a potluck or cook something easy. I think most people would rather spend the evening with friends they enjoy than with a stressed-out host fussing over an elaborate meal.

The perfectionist within might ask, "What's wrong with excelling?" Yet the desire for excellence differs from the desire for perfection. We can *excel* without having to *perfect*. Perfectionism is *a propensity for setting extremely high standards and being displeased with anything else*. Ironically, the anxiety created by the perfectionist's fear of failure can ruin the sought after pleasure of cooking an excellent meal for friends.

There is no reason you can't have *both* the desire to excel and the ability to accept and enjoy the moment, which may be less than perfect. So if you want, try to cook something great, but maintain a relaxed attitude despite anything that *might* go wrong.

You rarely hear about the perfect dinner party, but an over-spiced, smoke-filled, ridiculously-problematic dinner tale gets a lot of mileage in laughter-filled stories long after the smoke clears. Laughter is much better for your health and your relationships than the anxiety of having to achieve for *the* perfect outcome.

"How can I be happy when she's not?"

If misery loves company, what does happiness do? It turns out that happiness is infectious, at least between people married to each other. Recent research shows that married men are significantly more satisfied with their lives when their wives are happy with theirs, and vice versa.

British researcher Nick Powdthavee found that in married couples happiness can overflow from one spouse to the other, even for a partner who is facing difficulties.[2] Unfortunately, the same results were not seen among unmarried couples who live together.

In contrast, constant complaining or whining affects the happiness of one's spouse. Regularly pointing out flawed details in one's surroundings or relationships, like "the toaster is sticking again," can become a different message of "I am a pain to be around and will not stop complaining until you're as unhappy as I am."

It may seem obvious that it is more enjoyable to be with someone happy than angry or depressed. Yet this research gives people another good reason to seek happiness and not feel guilty about it. Since happiness is contagious, people can feel generous in welcoming happiness into their lives.

"Live in the now, not in the future!"

Live in the now?

While it may be trendy to live in the now, the emphasis on present-oriented living may be an exaggerated reaction to people living too much in the past or having high expectations of the future. If you succeeded in living purely in the present, you would have trouble maintaining a job, your relationships, and your wellbeing. You have to spend some time learning from the past and planning for the future to truly enjoy the present.

Time orientation

Most individuals are preoccupied with a particular time preference. Their focus on the past, present, or future is generally determined by cultural influence, upbringing, and personal experience. Each particular orientation has its benefits, but any one in excess can damage one's quality of life.[3]

1. Past Oriented

Benefit — People who focus on the past can enjoy the nostalgia of the past and feel connected to family, friends, and community through their memories. They can also learn from their past, and avoid repeating negative patterns while improving their lives. If their view of the past is positive — e.g., one of triumph or successful coping — they are likely to have positive expectations for the future.

Problem — People overly focused on the past may hold grudges, making it difficult to get beyond negative experiences. They may have a limited view of themselves and others based on past events. Dwelling excessively in the past also makes it hard to deal with the present or to plan for the future.

2. Present Oriented

Benefit — People who focus on the present can become mindful and self-aware. They are able to enjoy the moment, connect well with people, and experience pleasure and immediate gratification. They are often carefree and spontaneous. Being present in the moment, without the mental baggage of the past, can free a person from worries about the future as well as anger and regret about the past.

Problem — Studies show that people who are dominated excessively by a present orientation are found to be the least likely of the three types to be successful or to find fulfillment. Their inability to delay gratification can lead to reckless behavior, resulting in harm to themselves and others. Impulsive behavior — including addiction, promiscuity, and unethical behavior — ironically often leads to a future lacking in pleasure as well as security.

3. Future Oriented

Benefit — People who focus on the future are able to conceptualize long-term consequences, and thus avoid reckless behavior. They take care of their health and finances and are responsible to their family. Planning for the future often leads to a more secure, comfortable, and desirable future.

Problem — Too much planning for the future can lead to workaholism and worry. People who focus excessively on the future miss out on spontaneity, personal connections with other people, and present enjoyment of nature, beauty and pleasure.

How to Balance Time Orientations

Dwelling in any one specific time horizon — past, present or future — restricts overall happiness and effectiveness. Note that your first concern should be your present security. If you are being attacked by a grizzly bear, you won't be thinking about your IRA.

Ideally, we can balance all three time orientations with a healthy dose of each depending on the situation. Work may call for greater future orientation, while spending time with loved ones calls for more present orientation, and the lessons from the past may be more relevant when dealing with uncertainty.

It is when we lose sight of other time orientations that we get in trouble. When we make present-day decisions, we need to keep the future in mind — think about drinking and driving, over-eating, and other impulsive behaviors. Likewise, when we are at work or doing any kind of planning for the future, it is important to be in the present moment, so we can connect with the people we deal with, enjoy the small moments of beauty, and not let life pass us by. When we reminisce about the past, we need to make sure we don't get lost in memories and neglect present-day opportunities to live fully.

Live the Life you Desire

When we are aware of all time-orientations rather than getting completely carried away by one, life feels more embodied, whole and satisfactory. Learn from the past, live in the now, and consider the future.

---

[1] Dr. David Servan-Schreiber's video *Natural Defenses in Preventing and Treating Cancer.*

[2] Powdthavee, N. *The Happiness Equation: The Surprising Economics of Our Most Valuable Asset.*

[3] *The Time Paradox,* in which Philip Zimbardo & John Boyd discuss how the time-focus individuals emphasize greatly shapes how they think and act.

REFERENCES

Adler, A. (1927/1946). *Understanding human nature.* New York: Greenberg. New Jersey: John Wiley & Sons, Inc.

Arden, J. (2010). Rewire your Brain: Think your way to a better life.

Bly, R. & Woodman, M. (1998). The Maiden King: The reunion of masculine and feminine. New York: Henry Holt & Co. Inc.

Bohm, D. (1996). On dialogue. London, New York: Routledge.

Bowen, M. (1995). A psychological formulation of schizophrenia. Family systems: A Journal of natural systems thinking in psychiatry and the sciences. Vol. 2 Number 1.

Bowen, M. (1995). Clinical view of the family. Family systems: A Journal of natural systems thinking in psychiatry and the sciences. Vol. 2 Number 2, 153-157. (Original paper presented 1966)

Bowen, M. (1978). Family Therapy in Clinical Practice. New York: Jason Aronson.

Brazelton, T. (1992). Touchpoints: Your child's emotional and behavioral development. Addison-Wesley.

Brooks, D. (2011).The Social Animal: The Hidden Sources of Love, Character, and Achievement.

Campbell, J. (Ed.) (1971). The portable Jung. New York: Penguin.

Chaikin, A. L., & Derlega, V. J. (1974). Liking for the norm-breaker in self-disclosure. Journal of Personality, 42, 117-129.

Corbett, L. (2000). A depth psychological approach to the sacred. In: D. Slattery and L. Corbett (Ed.) Depth psychology: Meditations in the field (pp. 73-86). Zurich, Switzerland: Daimon Verlag.

Cushman, P. (1995). Constructing the self, constructing America. Reading, Massachusetts: Addison-Wesley Publishing Company, Inc.

de Mille, A. (1963). The Book of the Dance. New York : Golden Press.

Derlega, V. J. & Grzelak, J. (1979). Appropriateness of self-disclosure. In G. J. Chelune (Ed.), Self-disclosure: Origins, patterns, and implications of openness in interpersonal relationships. San Francisco: Jossey-Bass.

REFERENCES

Derlega, V. J. Harris, M. S. & Chaikin, A. L. (1973). Self-disclosure, liking and the deviant. Journal of experiential social psychology, 9, 227-284.

Douvan, E. (1977). Interpersonal relationships: Some questions and observations. In G. Levenger & H. L. Rausch (Eds.), Close relationship: Perspective on the meaning of intimacy Amherst: University of Massachusetts Press.

Dweck, C. S. (2006). Mindset: The New Psychology of Success. NY: Ballantine Books.

EMDR Institute, Inc. (2013). http://www.emdr.com/

Freire, P. (1999). pedagogy of the oppressed. New York: Continuum.

Freud, S. (1949). An outline of psycho-analysis. New York & London: W.W. Norton & Company.

Frey, R. (2008). Narcisstic Personality Disorder. In Encyclopedia of Mental Disorders. <http://www.minddisorders.com/Kau-Nu/Narcissistic-personality-disorder.html#ixzz1MooHWszB>

Fromm, E. (1973). The Anatomy of human destructiveness. New York: An Owl Book, Henry Holt and Company.

Goodchild, V. (2001). Eros and chaos: The sacred mysteries and dark shadows of love. York Beach, ME: Nicolas-Hays, Inc.

Gottman, J. (1999). The Seven Principles for making marriage work. New York: Three Rivers Press.

Gottman, J. (1994). What predicts divorce: The relationship between marital process and marital outcomes. Lawrence Erlbaum.

Gottman, J. (1994) Why marriages succeed or fail. New York: Simon & Schuster.

Gray, J. (1992). Men are from Mars, women are from Venus: A practical guide for improving communication and getting what you want in your relationships. New York: HarperCollins.

Gray, J. (1995). Mars and Venus in the bedroom: A guide to lasting romance and passion. New York: HarperPerennial.

Gray, J. (1994). Mars and Venus together forever: Relationship skills for lasting love. New York: HarperPerennial.

Grof, C. (1993). The thirst for wholeness. New York: HarperCollins Publishers.

Guggenbühl-Craig, A. (1977). Marriage: Dead or alive. Woodstock, CT: Spring Publications, Inc.

Hendrix, H. (1990). Getting the love you want. New York: HarperPerennial.

Hillman, J. (Fall, 1996). Marriages. Woodstock, Conn.: Spring Publications.

Hillman, J. (1976). Re-visioning psychology. New York: HarperPerennial.

Hillman, J. (1982). The thought of the heart & the soul of the world. Woodstock, Conn.: Spring Publications.

Hollis, J. (2001). Creating a life: Finding your individual path. Toronto, Canada: Inner City Books.

Hollis, J. (1998). The Eden project: In search of the magical other. Toronto, Canada: Inner City Books.

Johnson, C. Y. (2008). The joy of boredom. Boston Globe. http://www.boston.com/bostonglobe/ideas/articles/2008/03/09 /the_joy_of_boredom/?page=full

Jung, C.G. (1964). Man and his symbols. New York: Dell Publishing Co., Inc.

Jung, C.G. (1961). Memories, dreams, reflections. New York: Vintage.

Jung, C.G. (1971). Psychological types. In R. F. C. Hull (Trans.) The collected Works (vol. 6). Princeton, NJ: Princeton University Press. (Original work published 1921)

Jung, C.G. (1980). The archetypes and the collective unconscious. In R. F. C. Hull (Trans.) The collected Works of C. G. Jung (vol. 9) part 1. Princeton, NJ: Princeton University Press. (Original work published 1959)

Jung, C.G. (1981). The development of personality in R. F. C. Hull (Trans.) The collected Works (vol. 17). Princeton, NJ: Princeton University Press. (Original work published 1954)

Jung, C.G. (1972). Two essays on analytical psychology in R. F. C. Hull (Trans.) The collected Works (vol. 7). Princeton, NJ: Princeton University Press. (Original work published 1928 and 1943)

Kerr, M. & Bowen, M. (1988). Family Evaluation: The role of the family as an emotional unit that governs individual behavior and development. W.W. Norton & Company, Inc.: New York.

Klein, M. (1964). Love, guilt and reparation. In Klein, M. &Riviere, J. Love, hate and reparation. W.W. Norton & Company, Inc.: New York & London.

Klever, P. (1998). Marital fusion and differentiation, in P. Titelman (Ed.), Clinical applications of Bowen family systems theory, (pp. 119-145). New York: The Haworth Press, Inc.

Landmark Forum. (2013). http://landmarkforum.com/breakthrough-methodology/

Lerner, H. (1986). The Dance of Anger. NY: Perennial Library.

Levine, S. B. (1988a). Intrapsychic and individual aspects of seual desire. In S. R. Leiblum & R. C. Rosen (Eds.), Sexual desire disorders. New York: Guilford.

Luhrmann, B. (Director, Screenwriter). (1992). Strictly Ballroom (a film). Australia.

Malone, T. P., & Malone, P. T. (1987). The art of intimacy. New York: Prentice-Hall.

Moore, T. (1994). Care of the Soul. New York: HarperPerennia.

Powdthavee, N. (2010). The Happiness Equation: The Surprising Economics of Our Most Valuable Asset. UK: Icon Books, Ltd.

Prechtel, M. (March, 2003). Writers workshop (a workshop). Santa Barbara.

Riso, D.R. and Hudson, R. (1999). MD: The Wisdom of the Enneagram. Bantam Dell Pub Group.

Sardello, Robert J., and Severson, Randolph (1983). Money and the soul of the world. Texas: The Pegasus Foundation.

Schnarch, D. (1995). Audiotape: Empathy and differentiation. Evergreen, Colorado: Marriage and Family Health Center.

Schnarch, D. (1991). Constructing the sexual crucible: Paradigm-shift in sexual and marital therapy. New York: W.W. Norton & Company, Inc.

Schnarch, D. (May 2002). Lecture: Couples enrichment weekend. San Rafael, California.

Schnarch, D. (1997). Passionate marriage. New York: Henry Holt & Co.

Schnarch, D. (2002). Resurrecting sex. New York: HarperCollins Publishers, Inc.

Selye, H. (1956). The stress of life. New York: McGraw-Hill.

Servan-Schreiber, D. (2010). Natural Defenses in Preventing and Treating Cancer–a video. California: University of California Television. <http://www.youtube.com/watch?v=XaDt3AJQ98c&list=TLT5 qnXa-HjF7xgYeMUcaQAYWZR1TUhmKK>

Sixty Minutes (December 19, 2010). *Endless Memory*.

Somé, M. and S. (1994). We Have No Word for Sex: An Indigenous View of Intimacy (audio tape). Pacific Grove, CA: Oral Tradition Archives.

Somé, S. (1997). The spirit of intimacy: Ancient teachings in the ways of relationships. Berkeley, CA: Berkeley Hills Books.

Stone, H., Stone S., (1993). Embracing Your Inner Critic: Turning Self-Criticism into a Creative Asset. San Francisco: HarperSanFrancisco.

Stone, H., Stone, S. (1993). Embracing Our Selves: The Voice Dialogue Manual. Nataraj Publishing.

Stone, H., Stone S., (2000). Partnering: A New Kind of Relationship. Novato, CA: New World Library.

Tarnas, R. (1993). The Passion of the Western Mind. New York: Ballantine Books.

Tarnas, R. (2001). Depth Psychology. (Lecture). Carpenteria, California: Pacifica Graduate Institute.

Vaknin, S. (2007). Malignant Self-Love: Narcissism Revisited. Prague and Skopge: A Narcissus Publications Imprint.

von Franz, M. & Hillman, J. (1971). Jung's typology. Dallas, Texas: Spring Publications, Inc.

Wiseman, R. (2009). 59 Seconds: Think a little, Change a lot. London: Pan Macmillan.

Wiseman, R. (2003). The Luck Factor. NY: Random House.

Wigman, Mary (1963). The Language of Dance. Middletown, CT: Wesleyan University Press.

Winnicott, D. W. (1987). Babies and their mothers. Massachusetts: Addison-Wesley Publishing Company, Inc.

Winnicott, D. W. (1960). The theory of the parent-infant relationship. The International Journal of Psycho-analysis, 41, pp. 585-595.relationship. The International Journal of Psycho-analysis.

Wooden, J. and Jamison, S. (2007). The Essential Wooden. NY: McGraw-Hill.

Wooden, J. and Jamison, S. (2005). Wooden on Leadership. NY: McGraw-Hill.

Zafon, C.R. (2009). D. The Angels Game. New York: Doubleday, a division of Random House Inc.

Zimbardo, P. and Boyd, J. (2008). The Time Paradox. NY: Free Press.

INDEX

T

U

V

W

Y

Made in the USA
Middletown, DE
19 June 2016